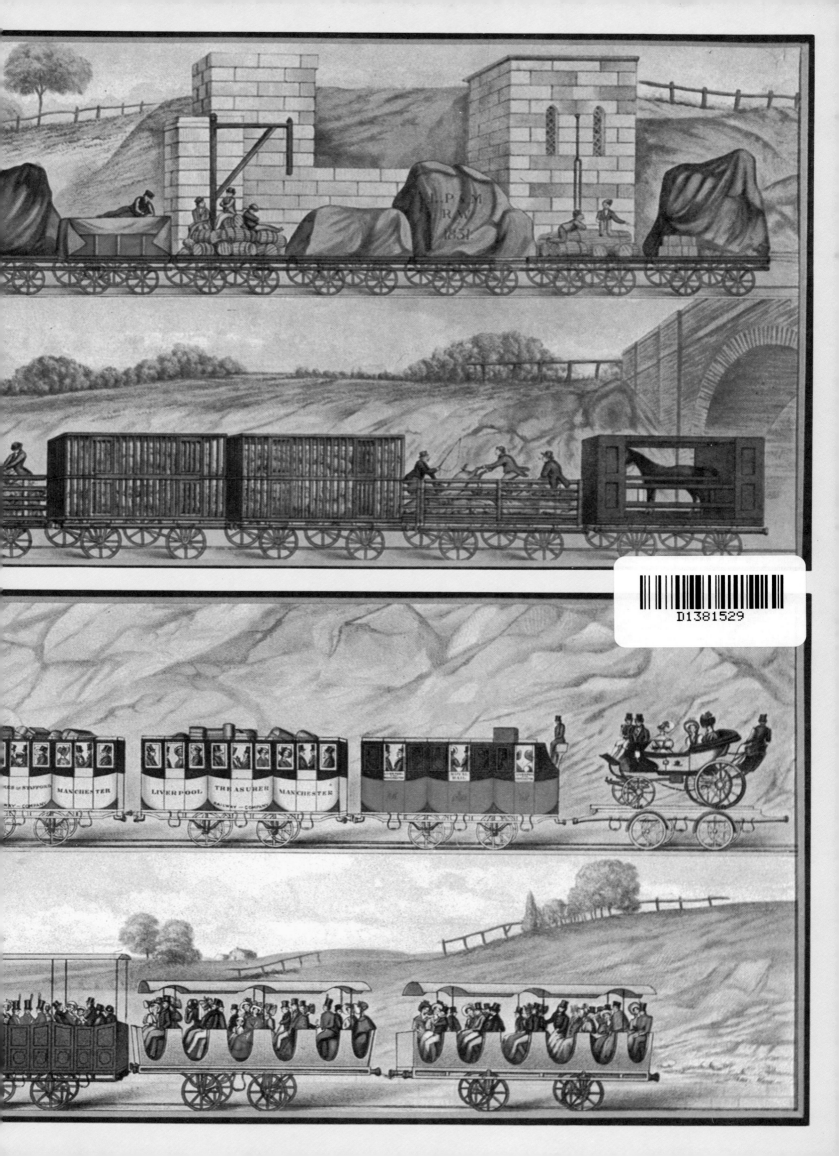

Endpapers
Varied rolling stock as used in the early
years of the Liverpool & Manchester
Railway. The superiority of the first class
trains can be seen in the third panel, which
also shows a predecessor of today's
'Motorail' and 'Auto Train'.

Page 1
A water-colour of the 1920s promoting long-
distance rail travel in continental Europe.

Page 2–3
A German Kriegslok silhouetted against the
skyline in Yugoslavia.

Page 4–5
A Prussian P8 4-6-0 hauls its coaches through
the Black Forest in Western Germany.

Steam

STEAM

John Westwood

Sundial

Contents

First published in 1980 by Sundial Books Limited
59 Grosvenor Street, London W1

Second impression, 1981

© 1980 Hennerwood Publications Limited

ISBN 0 906320 04 6

Produced by Mandarin Publishers Limited
22a Westlands Road, Quarry Bay, Hong Kong

Printed in Hong Kong

The Early Years

Steam railways existed long before the opening of the Liverpool & Manchester Railway in 1830 demonstrated so forcefully the possibilities of this form of transport. Leaving aside Trevithick's locomotive of 1804, which was the first successful steam locomotive although it never went into regular service, the Middleton Colliery near Leeds introduced steam locomotives for moving coal wagons as early as 1812, at the same time as the Napoleonic Wars were pushing up the cost of horse-feed. These lightweight locomotives, built by Matthew Murray, worked steam-driven cog wheels which engaged in rack teeth laid alongside one of the rails. These locomotives lasted about thirty years and were visited by, among others, George Stephenson. A pair of similar engines was built by the Berlin Royal Iron Foundry in 1816 while, at Wylam Colliery in Northumberland, William Hedley was building steam locomotives without a rack arrangement, believing that the smooth wheels would not necessarily slip on the equally smooth iron rails. His belief in the natural adhesion of iron against iron was

justified, and an important step forward was achieved. One of his locomotives, *Puffing Billy*, has been preserved and can be seen in the Science Museum in London.

George Stephenson worked as an enginewright at Killingworth Colliery, not far from Wylam. Widowed after three years of marriage, he entrusted his son Robert to the care of his sister, to enable him to continue with his job. After working hours, he took a few lessons in mathematics from the son of a neighbour, and this seems to have been the only schooling he ever received; everything else he knew was self-taught. He never learned to write properly, most of his letters and reports being written for him, and he never lost his Northumberland accent, which baffled most southerners. Ambitious, and confident of his practical ability, he compensated for his lack of education by giving his son the best he could afford. As a highly competent mechanic George Stephenson was well paid, so from the age of twelve Robert was despatched daily, on a donkey, to a private school in Newcastle whose other

pupils were distinctly middle-class. Robert did well, and later attended Edinburgh University. Thus at a critical period in railway development father and son would work as a team, George supplying the practical experience and business shrewdness and Robert the theoretical engineering knowledge.

While George Stephenson was at Killingworth, his employers asked him to build a steam locomotive for the colliery's railway. This locomotive, built in 1814, was *Blücher*, and was soon followed by *Wellington*. In *Wellington* the drive from the cylinders to the wheels was no longer through gears or pivoting beams but direct, through a connecting rod linking the piston with a crankpin offset from the wheel centre. This marked another milestone in the development of the locomotive, and was by no means Stephenson's last contribution. In the following few years Stephenson built more than a dozen colliery locomotives and in 1825, with his son Robert, he helped to found the firm of Robert Stephenson & Co, the world's first purely locomotive-building business.

Meanwhile the Stephensons had been engaged to engineer a much more ambitious colliery line, the Stockton & Darlington Railway. This, opened in 1825, was 25 miles long and intended to carry coal down to the coast. For this line the Stephensons built *Locomotion* and her three sister locomotives, only to discover that the unprecedented long runs meant that ordinary colliery-type locomotives soon ran out of steam. George Stephenson's last major contribution to locomotive design was *Experiment*, which was his answer to this problem. In this machine, boiler water tubes passed through the flue,

Below: On the threshold of world fame: George Stephenson in his late forties.

Below: Hedley's *Puffing Billy*, photographed at the end of its working career.

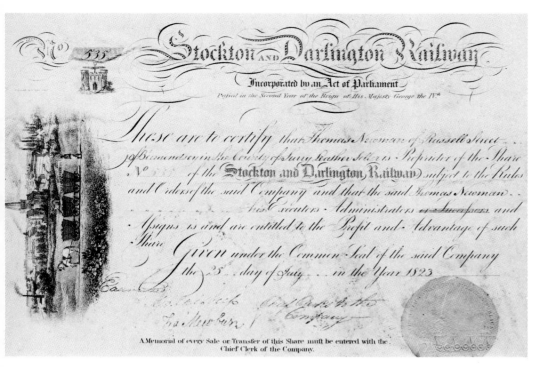

absorbing some of the heat from the exhaust gases on their way to the chimney. However, this device was difficult to maintain, and later locomotives used the firetube arrangement. This appears to have been a joint, or simultaneous invention of Robert Stephenson and the French engineer Marc Seguin (who, apart from importing Stephenson locomotives for his St Etienne to Andrezieux railway, was also making his own contribution to locomotive design and construction). In the firetube arrangement the gases from the firebox were drawn through narrow tubes which passed down the length of the boiler to the chimney, thereby transmitting further heat to the water.

While coal-hauling railways were experimenting with steam traction, inland transport, such as it was, remained in the hands of highway and canal companies. Neither of these provided a very good service, although the stage-coach companies, often in competition with each other, had some remarkably fast schedules, despite the poor state of the roads. Between Liverpool and Manchester, for example, the coach schedules at the time when the Liverpool & Manchester Railway was built had been reduced to two and a half hours for the run of about 32 miles. But the frequent number of accidents aroused much dissatisfaction on behalf of the public. For freight transport, a network of canals had been created, but these were operated as monopolies, imposing high rates and providing a rather poor service. It was this situation which led a group of dissatisfied Liverpool merchants to plan a railway to Manchester, and the result was the Liverpool & Manchester Railway, the world's first steam-operated common carrier (that is, public-use) railway.

Because of his successful participation in the Stockton & Darlington Railway, it was not surprising that the Liverpool merchants turned to George Stephenson when choosing an engineer. This was not a particularly creditable period in Stephenson's life, however. He became a member of a group which seemed to be attempting to gain a virtual monopoly of railway surveying, building, and engineering. Despite Stephenson's prestige, however, this monopoly was not achieved, although the careers of some very capable

Top left: A share certificate of the Stockton & Darlington Railway.
Centre left: The office and station of the Liverpool & Manchester Railway at Liverpool. The turntables for switching cars are in the foreground.
Left: A working replica of Stephenson's *Locomotion* at the Beamish Museum, County Durham.

engineers were damaged, sometimes destroyed, by Stephenson's refusal to recommend them for railway work. William James, the engineer who had drained Lambeth Marshes in London, had made an early survey for the Liverpool & Manchester line but Stephenson decided to make his own survey, which was inferior to James's. When Stephenson was summoned to give evidence to the parliamentary committee discussing the L & M Railway bill, he gave an impression of near-total incompetence. He did not know the width of the rivers the line was to cross, nor the depth, nor how many arches his bridges would need. Moreover, his calculations of heights and gradients proved to be incorrect. So abysmal was his showing that the Directors were obliged to withdraw their bill. They dismissed Stephenson as chief engineer. A chief surveyor Charles Vignoles, was hired and his survey, which was almost identical to James's, was readily accepted by parliament and the Liverpool & Manchester Railway Bill duly received the Royal Assent in 1826.

After this, Stephenson's allies among the directors of the company secured his reappointment as chief engineer, and he soon manoeuvred Vignoles into resignation; the latter, however, went on to a very distinguished career as railway-builder in many parts of the world. Henceforth the engineering of the L & M Railway was in the hands of the Stephensons, father and son, who acquitted themselves superbly. In particular, George Stephenson's determination to 'float' the line across the treacherous swamp of Chat Moss, despite opposition and criticism, justified itself. He poured masses of brushwood into this morass, eventually creating a foundation to which the roadbed could adhere.

At this period it was by no means certain that future railways would use steam traction. The virtue of the railway was that an iron wheel running on an iron rail aroused less friction than an ordinary wheel on an ordinary road. This meant that for the same expenditure of energy the load and speed could be greatly increased, a transport revolution in itself. The use of steam locomotives was a separate issue, and many intelligent observers believed that horse-power was superior to steam-power. A horse was more reliable, consumed local fuel, did not require trained mechanics, and when worn out its body could be used in all kinds of ways. The steam locomotive was ugly, noisy, smoky, liable to cause fires, to explode, and was quite brainless. Of

course, other arguments were used too. There were doctors who asserted that the high speeds which the steam locomotives might attain must be injurious, if not fatal. In Russia the Tsar's finance minister said that steam locomotives would consume as fuel the entire Russian forests, and some priests told their congregations that in the steam locomotive man was rashly trying to imprison the devil. It was the devil's efforts to escape that created all the noise, heat and steam, caused the pistons to move to and fro, and might end in tearing the boiler apart.

Those who advocated horse traction (and they included the directors of the Stockton & Darlington Railway, which used steam for freight but horses for passenger services) were not as obtuse as they are sometimes portrayed. In some circumstances horses were indeed superior to locomotives. The American Baltimore & Ohio Railroad, opened only a few months after the Liverpool & Manchester, was quite happy to use horses on its initial 13-mile line, hiring them cheaply from a stage-coach proprietor. Until quite recently British Railways used horses for shifting single freightcars in freight yards. A horse-worked branch connecting a state farm complex to the main line has recently been observed in Hungary.

In the 1820s and 1830s there was a third alternative, the use of fixed steam engines hauling trains by means of long cables. Steam engines not required to move themselves over rough and fragile track could be built more solidly, giving more power and reliability than the so-called 'travelling steam engines'. The need to change the cable as the train passed successive engine-houses was an obvious technical disadvantage,

and high speeds could not be achieved safely. Nevertheless the system was used for more than a century on steep inclines where a steam locomotive alone could not cope.

The directors of the Liverpool & Manchester Railway at first favoured cable haulage, considering the steam locomotive too uncertain in its performance. However, there was a pro-locomotive group among the directors which, appealing to the sporting instincts of Lancastrians, persuaded its hesitant colleagues to at least arrange competitive trials of various locomotives, with a prize for the best entrant. This competition (called an 'ordeal' at the time) was scheduled to take place at Rainhill, on a completed section of the Railway.

The Stephensons' entry for this competition was the *Rocket*, the latest creation of Robert Stephenson's locomotive works. This had 25 narrow copper tubes leading the exhaust gases from the fire through the boiler to the chimney, thereby increasing the amount of heat transferred to the water by these hot gases (which in previous designs had merely passed through one broad flue). The most serious competitor of the 'Rocket' was the *Sanspareil* of Timothy Hackworth, whose normal job was superintendent of the locomotives of the Stockton & Darlington Railway. A feature of the *Sanspareil* was the narrow pipe leading the exhaust steam to the chimney; this propelled the steam at a high pressure up the chimney, thereby creating a very strong draught for the fire and guaranteeing good steam-

Below: The 13-mile Baltimore & Ohio Railroad opened in 1830, using horses. The latter were changed at the half-way station.

raising capacity. A third entry was by Braithwaite and Ericsson (the latter subsequently designing the famous ironclad warship *Monitor* in the American Civil War). Their *Novelty* was a beautiful piece of machinery, its rather small vertical boiler being supplemented by mechanically worked bellows to maintain a very hot fire.

The trials of October 1829 attracted thousands of spectators, the wealthiest among them being accommodated in specially built grandstands. Each locomotive was required to pass before the judges backwards and forwards over a 1½-mile stretch of track twenty times, pulling a load of three times its own weight and 'consuming its own smoke'. George Stephenson described the *Novelty* as having 'no guts', and was vindicated when that locomotive's bellows caught fire, and it retired from the contest in a cloud of smoke. Timothy Hackworth had bad luck. He was not well-served by his workmen and his *Sanspareil* broke down on several occasions. In the end his boiler ran dry, the fusible plug in the firebox melted, and the luckless machine had to be towed away by hand amid a cloud of steam. The *Rocket*, thanks to its meticulous workmanship, performed faultlessly and on its final run George Stephenson forgot his usual caution, driving it at the unprecedented speed of almost 30mph. Moreover, this engine's fuel consumption, thanks to its multitubular boiler, was remarkably low. Thus the award of the £500 prize to the *Rocket* was quite justified, but not everyone was satisfied. For some, the fact that the competition was organized by the Railway, of which George Stephenson was chief engineer, made the award to Stephenson seem somewhat questionable. Even more interesting, after the competition was over some of the entrants continued running, and the repaired *Novelty* proved just as competent as the *Rocket*. The *Sanspareil*, with its steam blastpipe drawing its fire to white-heat, was very much a precursor of the heavy-duty locomotive, and could no doubt have exceeded the other entrants in terms of horsepower. But the blastpipe arrangement was still not perfect; although this locomotive did consume its own smoke, it did not consume its own coal, much of which was whisked, unburned, up the chimney by the ferocious draught.

Top left: An artist's impression of the Rainhill Trials. The Stephensons' *Rocket*, standing before the tent, is much more accurately shown than its rivals.
Left: The Rainhill competitors as shown in a contemporary account.

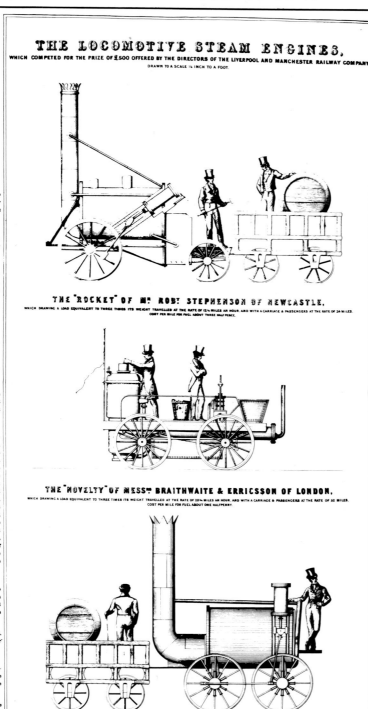

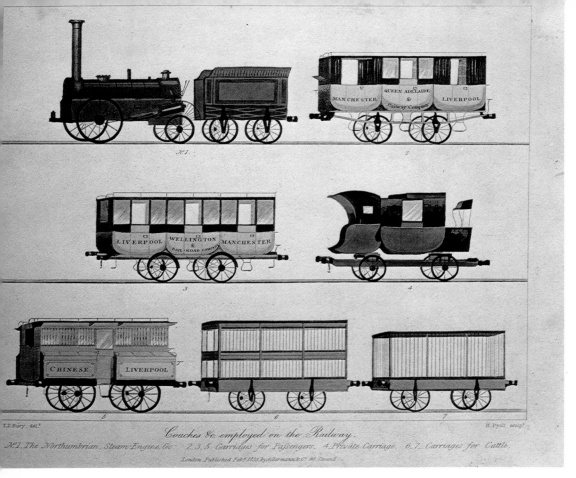

Coaches &c. employed on the Railway.
Nᵒ1. The Northumbrian, Steam-Engine, &c.   2,3,5. Carriages for Passengers.   4. Private Carriage.   6,7. Carriages for Cattle.
London Published Feb.ʸ 1833, by Ackermann & Cᵒ. 96 Strand.

Left: The different types of carriage accommodation offered by the Liverpool & Manchester Railway.

the two men. Having accomplished a handshake he wandered over the adjoining tracks, like many other guests, until another train was seen entering the station. Everyone hurried for shelter, pressing themselves against a wall or making themselves as small as possible between the two tracks. Huskisson was safely pressed against the Duke's car but, accident-prone since childhood, he changed his mind and moved when the *Rocket*, driven by Joseph Locke, was almost on him. He fell beneath this locomotive, and suffered a cracked thigh. The grievously injured M.P. was carried aboard the *Northumbrian* which was immediately despatched to the nearest town (Eccles) where there was a hospital. Driven by George Stephenson this locomotive reached 36mph, but there was no hope of saving Huskisson's life; he expired that evening, after having made a codicil to his will and uttering a farewell speech.

Immediately after the accident, the directors and the Duke conferred. The Duke of Wellington would have preferred to have cancelled the rest of the celebrations, but the directors said that the waiting Mancunians would surely riot if the expected trains and dignitaries did not appear. So the procession continued. However, the visit to Manchester was short. Many labourers and their wives were shouting unfriendly words, and projecting unfriendly gestures, at the Duke, so the trains were turned round as soon as possible and left for Liverpool. It had not been quite the glorious day that had been anticipated, but the Railway itself had little with which to reproach itself.

Although not the first railway, the Liverpool & Manchester was regarded as the 'Grand British Experimental Railway'. It fully justified this description, because it was the first railway to have as its object not a purely industrial purpose, but the winning of general, and moreover inter-city, traffic. It thereby became the prototype for the railway age. Not only did other British companies model their operations on those of the L & M, but visitors and commissions from all over the world came to the line or asked for detailed information. Men who had worked on this Railway were offered responsible positions on later lines, thereby sharing experience in practical ways. The opinion of the L & M directors was sought by Parliament when other railway proposals came up for scrutiny.

Thus the L & M's almost instant success assured the swift adoption of

One result of the trials was that the L & M directors decided to adopt the steam locomotive for their line, and Robert Stephenson produced a series of locomotives, each with detail improvements over its predecessor. With his *Northumbrian* the firebox for the first time was set inside the boiler shell instead of being merely attached to the boiler, and a true smokebox also appeared, at the chimney end.

Although trains had run earlier (and there had already been one fatal accident when a person unknown opened a switch and thereby derailed a train), the official opening was on 13 September 1830. That this was a really great occasion was evident from the long list of important personages invited to make the long and by no means easy journey to Lancashire. Foremost among them was the Prime Minister, the Duke of Wellington. Among others were Count Esterhazy, the Austro-Hungarian ambassador, Robert Peel, and Lord Salisbury. As guest of honour the Duke of Wellington was provided with his own carriage, an ornate vehicle covered with carved scrolls and surmounted by a canopy whose supports were hinged so that it could be lowered when passing through tunnels. Its upholstery was in rich crimson, and above it all was a ducal coronet. Enormous crowds had assembled, mainly to see the trains but also to witness any possible disturbances, for the Duke was highly unpopular in northern England. Grandstands had been erected, and as

the day approached all accommodation on the line was fully booked.

Eight trains, each with its own locomotive, were assembled in the Company's Liverpool yard to receive the guests, who exceeded 700. The Duke's train left first so that it could be free to go at the speed desired by the Prime Minister. Both tracks were to be used for this procession of trains. The ducal train consisted of only three cars: an open car for the band, the ducal car, and a car for the directors. The other trains were of from four to seven cars each. Running speeds varied from about 15 to 25mph and there was only one collision; this occurred when a locomotive wheel gave trouble and its train, having stopped, was rammed in the rear by the following train. This caused no casualties, but in fact one injury had occurred at the very start, when a cannon was fired to announce departure. The wadding from the blank charge struck a labourer standing nearby, and took his eye out.

But this accident was forgotten, overshadowed by a far more spectacular tragedy. It had been arranged that the trains would stop at Parkside station for water, and passengers had been asked to stay in their vehicles. Many ignored this advice, even though following trains were entering the station. William Huskisson, member of parliament for Liverpool and a former President of the Board of Trade, was taken to greet the Duke of Wellington and thereby ease a certain ill-will that had existed between railways elsewhere. But this success was not accidental. One factor was ample capital, permitting the laying of track and the purchase of rolling stock which were sturdier than some engineers might have considered necessary. With this very sound equipment the directors were well-placed to concentrate on their operating problems; the latter were many and varied because so many of the practices that are now routine all over the world had first to be worked out by trial and error.

One of the first problems was how to provide a freight service, competitive with the canals, yet without obstructing the passenger trains that provided most of the revenue? The solution, now so familiar that the original dilemma is difficult to recognize, was to run the passenger trains on schedules and to slip the freights through whenever the line was clear of passenger trains. Should a passenger train catch up with a freight, then the latter was side-tracked. If the freight's engineman failed to obey this rule, either from pride or independence of spirit, he was liable to dismissal. By 1840 there were usually about 15 daily freights operated by the Company, and certain precautionary routines (later copied by other lines) had been adopted. Employees along the line had been instructed to watch trains for signs of overhanging loads and for fire; the railway 'policemen' (signalmen) especially were enjoined to closely watch passing trains, a precaution that has persisted up to the present. But whereas the train fires in later times were usually caused by 'hot boxes' (overheated axle bearings), on the L & M it was locomotive sparks dropping into loaded wagons that was the problem. The solution was the adoption of the tarpaulin cover over open-top wagons, one more example of an L & M idea that became standard practice elsewhere. At the same time, the brakeman of each train began to ride on the last wagon, so that he could better observe the train.

It was the danger of fire that prompted the directors to prohibit smoking on the Railway's stations and in its first-class trains (the second class presented no problem, it was thought; the vehicles were so wind-swept that smoking was impossible).

Passenger traffic developed much faster than anticipated; in the first year of operation there were days when the line carried 2,500 people. Crowd control was then an unknown technique outside the army, and trains were delayed constantly because officials did not know how to ensure that all the passengers boarded the trains in time to make the scheduled departure. The adopted solution was to ring a large bell five minutes before departure, and a hand-bell just before the train left. This idea did not become wide-spread in Britain, for the guard's whistle was found to be better, but several European railways adopted it; the 'First Bell', 'Second Bell', and 'Third Bell', for example, were sounded on Russian stations well into this century.

The printed-card passenger ticket was unknown, and the task of selling places on the trains was handled by booking clerks writing out paper tickets in accordance with a seating plan of each train. The first commuting arrangement was agreed in 1842, when a traveller making six regular trips weekly was accorded a one-third fare reduction in return for buying six months' trips in advance. Free tickets were issued sparingly; the practice of allowing Company employees as much free travel as they wished was soon limited. One concession which was not widely imitated was the granting of free passage to local policemen in pursuit of criminals, on condition (a) that they established their identity and (b) that they actually captured their man.

Trains were either first or second class, and by the summer of 1836 twelve trains ran each way daily between Liverpool and Manchester, of these, four were first class. Third class was introduced in 1840, and was provided by building new second class vehicles, allowing the old second class to become third. For safety reasons, speeds were low; 17mph was the average speed for passenger trains in the first year. Enginemen could be dismissed if they covered the distance in less than the time allowed; one locomotive man escaped with a reprimand by claiming that he had been pushed by a following wind. But by the mid-1830s the first class trains ran from Manchester to Liverpool in 80 minutes but the second class was somewhat slower. Top speeds remained considerably slower than the locomotives' potential for the braking system was not adequate. Timetables at first consisted of lists of departure times from each terminus, passengers from the intermediate stations being expected to calculate their own departure times. When journey duration times were published the Railway made no guarantee that they would be maintained and this lack of any formal undertaking that schedules would be observed became characteristic of railways all over the world, and still remains so.

Accidents on the L & M were far more frequent than would be acceptable today, but thanks to the safety margins incorporated in the equipment fatalities due to material failures were quite rare. Locomotives did have a tendency to break their crank axles; existing metallurgical technology could not produce such axles with a sufficient margin to withstand the repeated thrusts of the connecting rods without risking an eventual failure, probably through a gradually widening hair line crack. But axle failures, and the occasional wheel fracture, did not generally result in casualties for speeds were low enough to permit derailments without catastrophic consequences. The frequently voiced fear of boiler explosions proved exaggerated and only two such explosions seem to have occurred during the L & M's existence. There were many more accidents and near-accidents caused by human error. Workers who hitherto had ridden nothing faster than a farm cart were sometimes found asleep on the trains they were supposed to be operating. On one occasion a train arrived in the Manchester terminus with its solitary engineman fast asleep and an embarrassing accident was avoided only by an observant porter, who jumped aboard and halted it. Because everything was so new, safety consciousness – the intuitive feeling of uneasiness when circumstances are leading towards a mishap – was at first absent. Even when it did develop, there was still the occasional case of drunkenness. The practice of enginemen 'signing on' when taking their locomotive from the depot, a routine which still seems to be practised everywhere, is said to have been a way of checking whether a man was sufficiently sober to sign his name. Dismissal for drunkenness on duty was quite common. Moreover in 1840 the directors' campaign against drunkenness was reinforced by an Act of Parliament which enabled railway officials to bring an employee found drunk on duty directly before a magistrate without the need for a warrant.

However, most injuries were caused by members of the public rather than by failures on the part of the railway staff. On the early trains, although the passengers knew they were travelling faster than they had ever travelled before, they could not quite conceive what this really meant until they stepped off a moving train to retrieve a hat which had blown off, or left a train between stations to save themselves a long walk. But eventually the bloodshed had its effect and passengers began to behave with more respect towards the

RAILWAY SIGNALS.

BIRMINGHAM—"ALL CLEAR."   "SLACKEN SPEED-ENGINE."   "CAUTION—RAILS."   DOVER—CAUTION—RAILS.

Obedience to the "signals" used on a railway is indispensable to the safe passage of a train. A moment's inattention to any one of their significant monitions may be followed by the instant death of heedless unsuspecting multitudes, while, on the other hand, a due observance of them at all times, in all seasons, by night as well as by day, divests the speed of even the fastest pleasure train of danger. It is, of course, most important that the servants of a line should become practically familiar with the things signified by the symbols used in their several establishments, but we also deem it to be of much consequence that the public itself should be acquainted with them, for, were such the case, we should cease to hear of the difficulty of obtaining evidence against negligent servants, which on occasions of accident has ordinarily prevailed. Every traveller would then be an observer and a judge of the means used for his preservation, and in proportion to the vigilance of his survey would be the attention of servants entrusted with duties so important to the lives and limbs of passengers.

The signals used on railways are of great variety. Most of the lines have systems peculiar to themselves; and, in consequence, no uniform observance prevails between them, which is a practice much to be regretted, as it tends to confuse the observation of men engaged on different lines, and of engineers who change one service for another. It cannot, however, be expected that so complicated an operation, and one, too, which has grown up under the management of independent companies, should speedily reach perfection. For the present, the signals are necessarily different on different lines; but we hope to see the day, when the set, which experience has proved the best, shall be universally and compulsorily adopted. We shall now describe the signals used on the more important lines.

Those observed on the London and Birmingham Railway demand the first attention. They consist of Police Signals—Signals shown at Intermediate Stations and the Long Tunnels; and the Engine Signals.

1. POLICE SIGNALS.—When the line is clear, and no obstruction in the way of the onward course of the train is either seen or suspected, the policeman stands erect, with his flags in his hand, but showing no signal. See Fig. 1. If it be required that the engine should slacken speed, and proceed with caution, from another engine having passed on the same line within five minutes, a Green Flag is held up in the manner shown in Fig. 2. If it be desired that the engine should slacken speed, and proceed with caution, from any defect in the rails, the Green flag is lowered, and held as shown in Fig. 3. But if it be necessary that the engine should stop altogether at any given point, a Red Flag is shown, and

2. SIGNALS SHOWN AT INTERMEDIATE STATIONS AND THE LONG TUNNELS.—Signal posts are erected on the "up" and "down" lines at the Intermediate Stations, and at the entrance of Primrose-hill, Watford, and Kilsby Tunnels, showing a Red Board of a large size, and a Green Board of a smaller size, as day signals. A Green or Red Light is substituted as night signals. On a train or engine passing an intermediate station, the Green signal is exhibited for the space of ten minutes, to denote that a train on the same line has passed within that period, and therefore due

caution must be observed on the part of the drivers and guards. On a train stopping at an intermediate station, the Red Signal is shown, and continued for five minutes after its departure, when the Green Signal is turned on, to complete the ten minutes' precautionary signal. On a train entering one of the tunnels, the Red signal is shown for the space of ten minutes, to prevent another engine entering within that time; unless the policeman can previously see through that the line is clear, when the Red Signal will be turned off, and the Green shown, to complete the ten minutes' signal. Should the Red Signal be shown

JUNCTION SIGNAL-MAN AT WORK.

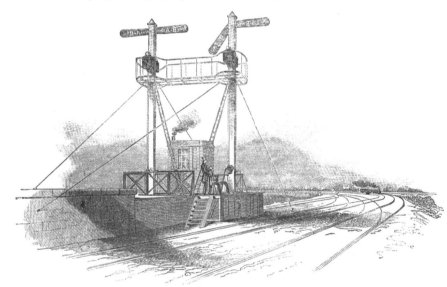

DOVER JUNCTION: DANGER: UP AND DOWN LINES, BRICKLAYER'S ARMS.   CAUTION, UP LINE; DANGER, DOWN LINE, LONDON BRIDGE.

waved backwards and forwards, the policeman facing towards the coming engine. A night the same signals are given, by means of coloured lamps. A White Light denotes the line clear: a Green Light requires the use of caution; and when the engine is required to stop, a Red Light is shown, but in place of being held steady, it is waved backwards and forwards. The engine-drivers and guards are, however, warned that any signal, either by day or night, violently waved, denotes danger, and a necessity of stopping.

an engine passing on that line is ordered invariably to stop on coming up to it.

3. ENGINE SIGNALS.—These consist of white and coloured boards by day, and white and coloured lamps by night, placed before and behind the train, to announce its character, whether it be on passenger, luggage, or special, service. The whistle is an important adjunct to the system, as it serves to give an almost irresistible warning, to all parties within reach of its shrill and earnest notes.

In giving orders for the use of these signals, the most imperative obedience is

enjoined on all parties concerned; but, at the same time, they are told not to rely on the signals being given at all times, but to exercise due and proper diligence, and on no account to be running before their proper time, or beyond their regular speed. The engine driver is also charged to stand by his "head gear," and to "keep a good look out."

In addition to these arrangements, a code of standing orders is issued, for precautions to be observed on the unexpected stoppage of an engine on the line and during fogs. For example:—Should any accident occur to cause the stop-

STATION POST SIGNAL—"CAUTION AND DANGER."

PLACING A FOG SIGNAL.

1844

dangers of the new mechanical age. In the meantime the Company suffered from various acts of vandalism: boys throwing stones at trains for amusement, adults with more serious motives placing obstructions on the rails. (The latter peril resulted in guard irons being fitted in front of the locomotives' leading wheels in order to push away such obstructions – one more instance of an expedient which became standard world-wide practice.) The most bloody accidents were collisions. Fog was also an early menace, but procedures were soon evolved to deal with this, including the protection of the rear of a stopped train by an employee running back to warn any following train. Some collisions also occurred because at a junction neither engineman of two converging trains would give way to the other; this was remedied by the threat of certain dismissal and possible arrest-warrant. Mis-setting of switches (points) could be punished in the same way, but this could hardly prevent over-tired pointsmen making the occasional fatal mistake. However, by finding some kind of remedy for each type of accident as it occurred, and by the evolution of a system of flag and light signals, the L & M did bring down the accident rate. In 1840 there were only eighteen accidents, and the three fatalities were not the fault of the Railway.

The L & M like other early railways was liable to the imposition of a criminal penalty known as the 'deodand' in the event of an accident. This could be imposed by the inquest jury whenever somebody died accidentally, without benefit of the last sacraments, and was intended to obtain recompense from the object that caused the accident, with the money going to charity or to a church which would offer prayers for the departed soul. In 1841, when a Great Western Railway train ran into a landslip, causing eight deaths, the locomotive concerned was penalized by a deodand of one thousand pounds. In this case the company made a successful appeal, and only a nominal sum was paid. The deodand (literally, 'to be given to God') was abolished in 1846 and one of the last occasions when it was levied on the railways occurred in that year, after a woman crossed the London & Brighton Railway's main line at Balcombe in front of an oncoming train; a railway policeman who tried to save her was also killed, and the jury imposed only a nominal deodand of one shilling on the locomotive.

The Liverpool & Manchester Railway proved such a success that its sponsors, railway-minded Liverpool merchants (forming with the Stephensons, the so-called 'Liverpool Interest'), were in an excellent position to dominate other big railway undertakings. The most serious rival of this Liverpool group was the Great Western Railway, which was mainly financed in Bristol and London and had a very original engineer, Isambard Brunel, in charge of its constructional and material departments. The GWR implicitly rejected many of the Liverpool standards, notably the 4ft 8½in (1,435mm) gauge. Brunel favoured a broader gauge, with its higher carrying capacity per vehicle and extra stability.

Technically the 7ft (2,133mm) gauge of the GWR was indeed superior to the Stephenson gauge, but it was the latter which triumphed by Parliamentary decision after it was realized that the division of Britain into two railway camps, which the existence of two gauges implied, would be a long-term handicap. Since one gauge had to be chosen, the greater mileage laid to the 4ft 8½in (1,435mm) standard meant that that gauge triumphed, but not before trials sponsored by the government had shown that Great Western locomotives could out-perform those of the Stephenson lines. Changing the gauge was a slow process; for many years the GWR was of mixed gauge, until in 1892 the last broad gauge train ran from London (Paddington) to the West of England. In the USA there was also a variety of gauges, lines in the south tending to be 5ft (1,524mm) and those in the north 4ft 8½in (1,435mm) and at one time it was possible to travel from New York to the Great Lakes over a line of 6ft (1,828mm) gauge. It was not until the first great transcontinental railway was authorized, on the 4ft 8½in (1,435mm) gauge, that the latter could be definitely regarded as the standard gauge in the USA to which all except the narrow-gauge railways soon conformed. Long before then a railway engineer from the southern USA, hired by the Russian Tsar, had persuaded the Russians to adopt the 5ft (1,524mm) gauge. In western Europe government supervision ensured that, except in Holland, there would be no gauge problems, but in various parts of the British Empire, especially India and Australia, several different gauges came into use, creating the present-day problem of arranging transhipment of

**Left: British railways signalling in the early 1840s.
Below: Isambard Kingdom Brunel.
Below right: A dramatised portrayal of the all-edge chaos at the break-of-gauge at Gloucester.**

Above: Floating the second span of the Britannia Bridge in 1849.

freight at break-of-gauge stations.

Technical questions were the province of a railway's chief engineer, whose appointment was a company's first important act after the preliminary proposals had been discussed and arrangements assured for raising capital. This was a crucial choice because on the engineer lay not only the responsibility of building a safe railway along the best alignment and as cheaply as possible, but also much of the 'political' work of the company. Getting a railway bill through Parliament was not easy, and a prestigious chief engineer, who could face cross-examination calmly and impressively, could make all the difference between a calm passage and the rejection of the bill. Parliamentary procedures were not cheap; in 1849 it was stated that the money spent on pushing railway bills through Parliament in 1845–47 would have been enough to build 500 miles of new line.

The burst of railway building in the 1840s might have been expected to reveal a shortage of capable railway engineers and in a sense it did, but this did not mean that inferior engineers very often were given work that was really too demanding for them. What seemed to happen was that a small number of experienced engineers managed to work through a greater number of railways, becoming engineers to several undertakings at the same time and delegating some of the more routine tasks to juniors. Men like the Stephensons, Brunel, and Locke

Above: The last broad-gauge train about to leave Paddington for the west in 1892.

would be in charge of projects both in England and abroad. Most of such men had gained experience in coal-mining; Brunel was an exception, but even he emerged from underground, his main experience having been in the construction of the Thames Tunnel.

What was especially notable with so many of the early chief engineers was their versatility; they could work as architects, bridge builders, locomotive designers, or interior decorators at the same time as they planned the alignment and construction methods of their railways. Robert Stephenson was a particularly notable locomotive builder and designer, a civil engineer who designed the routes of great undertakings like the London & Birmingham Railway, and the constructor of engineering monuments

like Kilsby Tunnel and the Britannia Bridge over the Menai Straits to Anglesey. In the case of the Kilsby Tunnel, where unsuspected water and unstable soil were encountered, it was only Stephenson's self-confidence which kept the project going to an eventual and expensive conclusion. In the case of the Britannia Bridge, he was willing to try and succeed with a novel construction for a novel problem; the length of this water crossing, together with Admiralty stipulations concerning minimum heights above water, led him to build a bridge consisting of two enormous metal tubes supported on masonry, a solution which endured successfully until the structure was damaged by accident after over a century of use. Brunel, too, was very versatile, although his innovatory zest led him into a number of spectacular failures; his locomotive designs, and his enthusiasm for atmospheric (pneumatic) railways were among his failures, but he will be remembered for the superb engineering of the Great Western Railway and for his bridges. His Royal Albert Bridge at Saltash, taking the railway from Devon into Cornwall, is still in use, its construction (a tubular arch from which the track is suspended) having proved stout enough for loads several times heavier than those anticipated at the time of its construction in the 1850s. But perhaps Brunel's most notable bridge is the brick viaduct over the Thames at Maidenhead, carrying the first section of the Great Western Railway and designed in the 1830s. The arches of this bridge were so flat that laymen could hardly believe that a train could pass without it collapsing, but it still stands. Brunel was also a great protagonist of the timber viaduct, but these have now all disappeared. Elsewhere in Britain (and in France later) long high railway viaducts of brick or stone began to cross deep valleys; at first regarded as outrageous eye-sores, they are now treasured as graceful monuments of the 19th century.

The first task of a new railway's chief engineer was the search for the best route between the towns that were to be connected. In the 1830s he would arm himself with Ordnance Survey maps and walk or ride over the intervening country, accompanied by an entourage of assistants. During the survey for the London & Birmingham Railway, Robert Stephenson is said to have walked twenty times between the two cities. Gradually the engineer would build up in his mind a feasible picture, which he would confirm by asking his assistants to 'take the levels' for the various contours to be negotiated. Having worked out an ideal route, the engineer then had to change it here and there to allow for strong opposition on the part of powerful landowners or corporations. When Northampton traders wished to persuade Stephenson to route his London & Birmingham Railway through their town he was deterred by opposition from the local landowners and stuck to his original intention of passing well to the westward. In 1834 the Great Western abandoned its intention of building a branch to Windsor, following opposition from Eton College. The Eton headmaster claimed that 'Our objection arises from the danger which we think will result to the lives of the boys. It will be impossible to keep the boys from the railroad in their hours of liberty. I may also say that the passengers themselves will be placed in a situation of great danger in consequence of the thoughtless tricks which the boys will play . . .' In France,

because of local opposition the main line of the Paris-Orleans Railway did not enter Orleans nor, when it was extended to Bordeaux, was it allowed to enter Tours. All kinds of reasons were advanced against the railways; they would bring dissolute strangers to a locality, their smoke would discolour the wool of the local sheep, but essentially it was the customary fear of something both significant and new. Not all the objections were unreasonable; landowners had some justification for regarding new railways as a blot on the landscape particularly when they cut through hitherto unspoiled countryside.

As soon as the compromise between the ideal and the feasible route was arrived at, the engineer's assistants and surveyors made new and more accurate surveys. From these, relevant parts were copied and sent to county clerks and other interested parties. The different parishes and landowners received details of the land required and the maximum heights of cuttings and embankments. After this, quite an expensive undertaking in itself, the chief engineer was required to speak for the railway's bill when it came before Parliament. If it was passed (and often it was not; some railways had to go through the process several times), the engineer could at last settle down to the detailed construction of his line: the choice of gradients and exact alignment, the requirement for bridges, the amount of earthworks (taking care that embankments should approximately equal cuttings, so that the spoil removed from the latter could be utilized for the former). After trial borings to determine the strata of cuttings and tunnels, a cost estimate was prepared and then the work was put out for contract.

The usual practice was to divide the line into sections, and engage a different contractor for each. The lowest bid was not always accepted for the determining factor was often the likelihood of the bidding contractor being in a position to actually carry out his undertakings. Many contractors went bankrupt, and some committed suicide, during the course of their work, which could mean that a given section of line fell badly behind schedule. This in turn would mean that the railway could not be opened, and until it was, the money invested in it produced no return. Contractors themselves divided their allotted length into sections, which they then sub-contracted. In turn the sub-contractors engaged gangs of 'navvies' under an elected 'ganger' to carry out the labouring work.

As the years passed, the smaller and financially weaker contractors

Above: Thomas Brassey, one of the really big railway contractors.

disappeared, but a new breed of big railway contractors emerged. Of these, Thomas Brassey was perhaps the best-known. Responsible for many railways in Britain and overseas, he began by acting as contractor for the engineer Joseph Locke and built, among others, the Grand Junction and the London & Southampton railways. In the 1840s he built the Paris-Rouen and Havre-Rouen lines in France, and also participated in the Grand Trunk of Canada, and lines in Australia, India, South America, and Europe. He was financially so powerful that he could sometimes help to finance the railways he was engaged to build, and he was also able to manipulate the companies. One of his coups was to build a direct line to Portsmouth, which he then offered to the highest bidder among the three companies already competing for the London-Portsmouth traffic. At the height of his power he employed 75,000 men, and it is estimated that he participated in the building of 1,700 miles of railway in Britain and another 3,000 miles overseas. His lines were usually well-built, and the Paris-Havre main line in France still shows his influence. However, it was not long before the French began to dispense with British help in railway building and operation.

By the late 1840s the shape of Britain's mainline network could already be discerned. In 1846 the London & North Western Railway had been formed by the merging of the London & Birmingham, the Manchester & Birmingham, and the Grand Junction railways; the Grand Junction was itself a recent amalgamation and included, notably, the old Liverpool & Manchester. The Manchester & Leeds

Above: Stephenson's *Der Adler* opens the Bavarian Nürnberg-Fürth Railway in 1835.

Railway had become the Lancashire & Yorkshire, destined to be one of two great regional British railways (the other was the North Eastern, not yet formed, which would include the Stockton & Darlington among its constituents). Another great British railway, the Midland, already linked Derby, Birmingham and Bristol. The Great Western Railway joined London and Bristol, and worked closely with the Bristol & Exeter Railway to provide a main line to Devon. The London & Southampton Railway was flourishing, and destined to be the nucleus of the London & South Western Railway. The London, Brighton & South Coast Railway had lines south of London which over the years would develop into a great passenger railway. In Scotland the Caledonian Railway had built over Beattock Summit to connect Carlisle and Glasgow.

In France, early railway history was rather different. There had been a horse-drawn colliery line of some length built in the 1820s near

St Etienne, and in 1830 the St Etienne to Lyons Railway was begun. By 1831 this line had steam locomotives and also ran a passenger service. But because in France anything which happened outside Paris was not deemed worthy of attention, these successful lines had a negligible effect on public opinion ('public opinion' also being exclusively Parisian). In the 1830s much of the public 'discussion' of railways took literary forms, ranging from poems to music hall songs, most of which referred to the English, not the French, pioneer railways. Thus in an 1836 'science fiction' novel, *The Picturesque Travels of Kaout't-couch*, action takes place on 'The Island of Civilization', where railway trains are not propelled by steam but by electricity, and are so rapid 'that it is physically impossible to distinguish the moment of arrival from the moment of departure'. But apart from poets, songwriters, journalists, and a handful of philosophers who argued that governments should spend on railways the money which otherwise they would waste on armaments, there was little influential interest in railways. It was the Péreire brothers who

changed all this. Realizing that nothing would be done until Parisians had a railway of their own to play with, they built the Paris-St Germain line. This was short (thereby conserving capital), went to a place where Parisians could enjoy themselves, and took a direction which would make worthwhile a future extension. This line opened in 1837, in the presence of Queen Marie. It immediately became a great attraction and one of the sights of Paris. What is more, it achieved the Péreires' original intention, arousing a public clamour for more railways. By 1842, after five years of intermittent but stormy debate, the National Assembly passed its Railway Law and thereby determined the future shape of the French railway network. This authorized the construction of a system radiating from Paris, with only two cross-country lines which would not touch the capital (Marseilles-Bordeaux and Dijon-Mulhouse). Companies were to be assisted by the government, in return for close government control. In Germany, still a collection of independent states, the first line, from Nuremburg to Fürth, was opened in 1835, sponsored by King Ludwig and powered by a Stephenson locomotive, *Adler*. Four years later a true main line was opened, from Leipzig to Dresden, which prospered and encouraged other ventures. However, it was not until the 1840s that the largest state, Prussia, completed its first lines, beginning with the Magdeburg-Leipzig railway. In the USA, like Britain, railway construction followed no plan and was usually sponsored by commercial interests intent on boosting their own localities. The Baltimore & Ohio Railroad, like the St Etienne-Lyons Railway in France, was opened in 1830, soon after the Liverpool & Manchester Railway and its success did much to encourage further ventures. However, the B & O was initially only 13 miles long; its great days were yet to come. After the B & O the next common-carrier railroad was the South Carolina & Charleston, which was the first to use steam traction on a daily basis. Expansion was rapid in the 1830s, and it was possible by 1838 to travel from Washington to New York by a succession of trains operated by several different companies. Five years later passengers between Boston and Buffalo, a distance of about 500 miles, used the rails of nine separate companies.

Most companies bought their locomotives from independent builders, although a few British railways had workshops in which they built their own. On the London & Birmingham Railway, locomotive affairs in the early years were in the hands of a locomotive builder, Edward Bury, whose firm hired its locomotives to the Company. These were of the 'Bury' type, rather small for the time, with bar frames and the 'haystack' firebox (so called because it was tall, round and round-topped, like haystacks of that period). As such, these engines represented a variation and competitor to the Stephenson engines and some were exported to the USA, where the bar frame found immediate and lasting favour. However, the L & B used these locomotives long past the time when they were adequate and often three or more locomotives were used on a train, which was a very uneconomical practice. Another distinct line of locomotives was taking shape on the Great Western Railway, where the broad gauge engines built at the Company's Swindon Works were operated on the world's fastest schedules.

In Newcastle the firm of Robert Stephenson remained the most experienced, and still perhaps the most innovative, of the locomotive builders. The *Rocket* type was soon obsolete, being superceded by the six-wheel

Above: The Camden (London) freight station of the London & Birmingham Railway. One of Edward Bury's typically small locomotives, with 'haystack' firebox, awaits its train.

Planet type, in which the cylinders were placed underneath the smokebox between the frames, driving a cranked axle. It was this design which several of the new American railways imported, but although the workmanship was good the design was rather unsuitable for the light and tortuous tracks of American lines. It was not long before Americans began to develop their own designs on the basis of the British engines. In 1832 John B. Jervis introduced a new wheel arrangement. This had a single pair of driving wheels with, in front, four smaller wheels arranged in a leading truck that could swivel. With no carrying wheels at the rear, this wheel arrangement was described as 4-2-0, and provided a very flexible wheelbase. By 1840 most American locomotives were of this wheel arrangement, and some were exported to Europe by the locomotive building firm of Norris; even Britain's Birmingham & Gloucester Railway bought some. But by the mid 1840s the type had been superceded in America by the 4-4-0, which was destined to be the American standard, decade after decade, for both freight and passenger work.

Meanwhile Robert Stephenson had introduced his *Patentee* series, of the 2-2-2 wheel arrangement and generally similar to the *Planets*, having massive plate frames both inside and outside the wheels. Then, in 1841, came Stephenson's 'long-boiler' concept. The long boiler of this three-axle design was intended to absorb a greater proportion of the heat from the hot gases passing through the boiler tubes on their way to the chimney. The boiler overhung the wheelbase considerably, causing some

stability problems for the passenger (2-2-2) version. The freight (0-6-0) version was very successful in continental Europe, where it was known as the 'Bourbonnais' type because that area in France was the scene of its first successes over heavily graded line.

Although Robert Stephenson's works would maintain a substantial export business into the middle of the next century, British builders only very briefly enjoyed a monopoly of locomotive construction. The first German-built locomotive (admittedly a Stephenson inspiration) was the *Saxonia* of 1839, and in 1841 three famous German builders started business (Maffei, Kessler, and Borsig). Soon most of the larger German states had their own locomotive building companies. In France, locomotives were mainly home-built, although it was not until the 1850s that a truly French school of design broke away from the British tradition. In the USA, several mechanics with experience of assembling British locomotives started their own workshops, some of which built a few machines and then disappeared while a few developed into very large firms. The Norris brothers for a decade or two had great success, and even opened businesses in continental Europe. A more solid reputation was achieved by Matthias Baldwin, whose Baldwin Locomotive Works survived into the diesel era.

For carrying passengers, the rigid wheelbase four-wheeler was the type of vehicle favoured by the early British

Above: A model of Stephenson's *Planet* type locomotive in the Science Museum, London.

railways. The body, being initially built by coachbuilders, naturally followed the design of stage coaches. In time this was modified; for example, the coachbuilders soon discovered that several bodies might be mounted on one chassis, thereby creating the compartmented vehicle. On the first railways, private carriages were also allowed, provided they met certain technical and safety standards. The ordinary road coach, mounted on a flat railway car, was also seen. However, the Liverpool & Manchester Railway, among others, wished to attract more of a mass market than could be provided by those few who could afford to travel in stage-coach conditions. Hence the introduction of second class vehicles, which at first had little protection from the weather. These could accommodate many more passengers than the first class, and although fares were considerably lower the revenue per vehicle was higher for second than for first class (a feature that was to be typical of almost all railway passenger services). At first, too, the first class vehicles were assembled into first class trains that stopped only at first class stations; only the second class trains with their second class vehicles stopped at all stations. In accordance with coaching tradition, for many years first class passengers were said to travel 'inside' and second class 'outside'.

Third class appeared in the mid 1830s. The Stockton & Darlington, for example, introduced it in 1835. Whereas first class rail travel had been designed to attract the stage coach passenger, and second class to attract passengers formerly travelling by cheaper road conveyances, third class, on the S & D and other railways, was aimed at the poorer traveller who hitherto had made his journey on foot. Thus the third class fare was very low, and the third class vehicle little more than an open freight car, often without seats so as to accommodate as many passengers as possible. However, in the early 1840s the most primitive kind of third class vehicle was already disappearing. The big step forward for the third class passenger came with 'Gladstone's' Railway Act of 1844. Among other things, this compelled companies to run daily, in each direction, at least one train which would serve all stations, average no less than 12mph (19km/h), charge not more than one penny per mile, and consist of vehicles which would protect passengers from the weather. In return, the duty payable on passenger receipts would not be levied on these trains. This last concession gave the Board of Trade, which supervised the Act, a better weapon than legal action, for recalcitrant companies did not wish to forfeit their right to this remission. In several cases, especially on questions of accommodation standards, the Board was able to persuade companies to do a little more than the Act strictly required. The broad result of the Act was a higher standard for third class travel, but the exact effect differed from company to company. On the Great Western, for example, the requirement to provide covered accommodation for third class travellers virtually obliged that Company to do at least as much for the second class, who had hitherto also been provided with open cars.

Because British track was well laid, with curves of generous radius, the four-wheel car's rigid wheelbase did not jolt the passengers excessively. In continental Europe, also with solidly engineered lines, similar cars were used. These later developed into the rigid wheelbase six-wheeler, which survived in Britain until the 1950s, and whose modern version can still be seen in central Europe. In America, however, the same track conditions that had proved unsuitable for British locomotives also determined the emergence of a specifically American type of passenger vehicle (and of freight car, too, for it was not long before the four-wheel rigid wheelbase freight car was replaced by the box-car, running on two four-wheel trucks). The American style of car was uncompartmented, being of the so-called saloon layout with a central gangway. The two swivelling trucks which supported the body enabled it to negotiate short-radius curves and also permitted a much longer vehicle. The open layout, and the provision of end platforms at each end of the car with the central gangway connecting them, gave American passengers, usually making longer journeys than their European contemporaries, much more opportunity to stretch their legs.

In most countries at the beginning of the railway age there was a great variety between the services and practices of the different companies. In many aspects this difference has continued up to the present, in those countries where the railways have not been absorbed into a single state undertaking. For example, in Britain in the late 1830s the London & Birmingham Railway's trains were regarded as clearly inferior in comfort to those of the Grand Junction, a difference which was eventually eliminated by the merging of these two companies into the London & North Western. However, the standard of the L & B trains were quite acceptable for railway travel at that time. The 'mixed' trains of that Company comprised first class vehicles with six cushioned seats, all seats being numbered, together with second class vehicles, open sided but roofed, providing eight uncushioned and unnumbered seats. However, the 'Night Mail' included second class vehicles which were 'entirely protected from the weather'. Third class vehicles on this railway, used only in slow stopping trains, were quite uncovered and had benches seating four passengers each. In the 1840s a few companies introduced fourth class, which was extremely cheap, although the passengers were required to stand, closely packed, in open vehicles.

By the mid 1840s the London & Birmingham line, having become the southern division of the London & North Western, was operating rolling stock which was already designed in the railway, as opposed to the coaching,

tradition. An eye-witness account of 1849 speaks of the quite intensive train service operated from the London terminus at Euston and the care lavished on the coaching stock. '. . . as soon as an up-train arrives . . . while it is still in motion, and before its guard – distinguished by a silver-buckled black shiny patent-leather belt, hanging diagonally across the white buttons of his green uniform-coat – has ventured with practised skill to spring from the sideboard of the train to the platform, two greasy-faced men in canvas jackets, with an oil-can in each of their right hands . . . are to be seen running on each side of the rails below in pursuit of the train; and while the porters, holding the handles of the carriage doors, to prevent any traveller from escaping, are still advancing at a brisk walk, these two oilmen, who have now overtaken the train, diligently wipe as they proceed the dust and perspiration from the buffer-rods of the last carriage.' These oilmen then proceeded down the train, cleaning and polishing the buffer-rods, closely followed by another pair who opened the flap of each axle-box to refill the latter with the bearing lubricant, a special mixture of tallow and palm-oil. Meanwhile the carriage 'searcher' was lifting the cushions and carpets of every compartment in search of passengers' belongings, which in due course would be registered and stored for claiming at the Lost Luggage Office. On the train roof a 'strapper' examined each luggage strap, cleaning and greasing it and replacing any which seemed weak (a precaution carefully

Below: *Pioneer*, a Baldwin locomotive of 1836, and the first in Chicago.

followed because of unhappy experiences with heavy items breaking loose while trains were travelling at full speed). When these operations were completed, the stationmaster ordered the vehicles to be removed, either by the station's pilot locomotive or by means of small turntables set in the arrival tracks, over which individual carriages could be switched to a parallel storage track (such storage tracks can be seen in many old prints of the early railway terminals). When the vehicles arrived in the storage track, '. . . a large gang of strong he-housemaids, clattering towards them in wooden shoes and in leather leggings rising above their bony knees are seen advancing. . . . Half a dozen dusty, dirty-faced, or rather dirty-bodied, carriages are simultaneously assailed on each of their sides by wet mops flying up, down and around in all directions. . . . It may possibly not be known to some of the most fashionable of our readers that among ''moppers'' there exist the same gradations which so distinctly separate other classes of society. A ''first-class mopper'' would on no account demean himself by mopping a second-class carriage, and in like manner a ''second-class mopper'' only attains that distinction after he has for a sufficient length of time been commissioned to mop horse-boxes and common luggage-trains'. After being thus washed and dried so that their varnish glistened, the vehicles were examined by a coach foreman and then, finally the 'duster' arrived with his cloth, leather, dust-pan and brush. When he had finished cleaning the compartments the vehicles were ready to be marshalled to form a departing train.

The Company Age

By the 1870s the British and West European networks were largely complete, but this was not true elsewhere in the world, for many of the great railways were yet to come. In 1869 the first American transcontinental line was finished, but other great transcontinentals, like the Canadian Pacific, Trans Siberian, and Trans Australian railways were still only being talked about. Even in Britain and Western Europe the building of secondary lines continued. Ceremonies marking the beginning and the end of the construction of a new railway were no less elaborate than in the early days, although rather less newsworthy except in those localities being joined for the first time with the railway system. In most countries, 'turning the first sod' usually marked the start of construction, the appropriate square of turf being lifted by a local dignitary, sometimes

with the help of a silver spade and, more rarely, a silver wheelbarrow. This comparatively simple act did not always go smoothly. Sometimes the sod proved resistant to a mayor too long unaccustomed to physical labour, and on the North Staffordshire Railway's great day the ceremonial spade bent double under the strain.

The really big celebrations were reserved for the completion of a line. In France the ceremony might include the blessing of the locomotive by the local priesthood. In America there was the ceremony of driving the last spike. The latter was often of gold or silver, and was removed a few seconds after it had been driven in, to forestall thieves. When in 1869 the Central Pacific and Union Pacific railways met head-on at Promontory in Utah, thereby completing the first American transcontinental, trains of dignitaries were brought to

witness the last spike ritual. In this case there were two golden spikes, one to be driven in by each president of the two railroads. Both these gentlemen missed their target on the first swing of the silver sledgehammer, but eventually the spikes were driven home. The cross-tie into which they had been driven was promptly removed, together with the spikes, and one spike has survived in the Stanford Museum, together with the silver sledgehammer. As for the last cross-tie, made specially of laurel wood this was replaced in the railway by a succession of replicas, each of which was stolen in turn and chopped into small pieces to be sold as genuine relics.

In other countries an inaugural train and a sumptuous banquet marked the occasion. Often several banquets were held simultaneously for the respective social divisions. Dignitaries, engineers,

Below: One of the best-known railway pictures: the last-spike ceremony at Promontory, Utah, in 1869. In the centre the Union Pacific's inaugural train from the east touches the Central Pacific's train from the west.
Bottom: Third class travel in continental Europe, in a nominally five-a-side compartment.

and promoters would sit at one, lesser officials at another, and at separate inns refreshments would be provided for the railway's and the contractors' labourers. The most important guests would travel on a special inaugural train, whose first car would be an open wagon to accommodate a brass band playing appropriate tunes like 'See, the conquering hero comes!'. At the end of the line the train would disgorge its passengers, who would proceed to a great tent or to a nearby hall to drink a toast to the Queen, listen to self-congratulatory speeches, and heartily enjoy the lavish spread provided at the expense of the railway company. This great opening was often the last occasion when it could afford to be generous. But not every company succeeded in making the right impression, however. When the Ipswich to Norwich line was built, the mid-way

town of Stowmarket was chosen for the celebrations, with inaugural trains starting from each end and meeting at that town. Unfortunately the train carrying dignitaries from Ipswich arrived an hour before that from Norwich, so the Norwich people found the banquet three-quarters consumed by the time they arrived. When the Geelong to Melbourne line was opened in Australia the company ordered $5\frac{1}{2}$ tons of poultry and meat, $\frac{3}{4}$ ton of fish, $\frac{3}{4}$ ton of pastries, and $\frac{1}{2}$ ton of ices and jellies for its guests. However, the Melbourne party found that all the trains to the place of festivity were packed tight with passengers from Geelong and they were obliged to stand for hours under a grey sky in mud 'over which the patent leather boots of military volunteers made a profound impression'. Eventually an empty train was provided for them but they arrived only as the feast was ending. 'It would be difficult to produce a greater failure . . . or a more discreditable scheme of management' was the verdict of the Melbourne newspaper.

In Britain, new lines built after 1870 were mainly those railways destined to be little used and to be the first victims of the line abandonment policies of British Railways in the 1960s. There were some exceptions; some cut-off lines to shorten existing main routes were among these, and also some lengthy lines in Scotland. British train speeds at this period were higher than those of other countries; only the USA seemed likely to rival Britain, and then only on a few lines that were suited to high speed. Whether the British railways were efficient is another matter. They certainly had many critics. Why they were unpopular is uncertain, but among the causes must have been the accident rate (or rather, the fact that accidents were well publicized in a period when newspapers were beginning to be widely read). There was, also, the occasionally arrogant attitude of lower railway officials to their customers, an attitude all too easy to adopt at a time when the railways had a virtual monopoly of land transport.

In Britain, as in the USA, government planning of the railway network was not favoured. True, in the 1840s there had been a brief attempt by the Board of Trade to impose restrictions on railway building with the aim of ensuring that all important places were served and that there were not too many railways linking the same towns. But the prime minister (Peel) had not pressed the Board's scheme. Moreover, in its 1844 Railways Act the government had seemed to imply that 10 per cent

dividends would be achieved by railway companies, and this encouraged railway promoters to suggest new lines, while making investors only too happy to put their money into the new form of transport. A rush, almost a panic, ensued as infant companies hurried to raise money and submit their bills to Parliament; a bill which had the good fortune to be approved by both houses of Parliament was regarded almost as a licence to print money. At the close of 1845 no fewer than 788 railway bills were awaiting parliamentary scrutiny. This burst of railway promotion and building was accompanied by laxity in accounting which in several cases led to fraud, or to the loss of capital through over-optimism or incompetence. This 'Railway Mania' ended, disastrously for many investors, in 1847; an economic recession, followed by a tightening of credit, caused a precipitous fall in the values of most railway shares.

The lessons of the Mania were partially learned, in the sense that investors were henceforth more cautious, but railway construction continued at a fast rate nevertheless. Companies strove to carve out for themselves their own territories, by opposing the approach of other lines, while at the same time extending their own lines in the hope of drawing traffic away from their neighbours. The first battles were fought in Parliament, where opposition could be mustered against new railway bills. At the same time, alliances were also formed with other railways; sometimes these went as far as amalgamations to produce one powerful company out of several small enterprises, others were of the 'if you don't build to city X, we won't build to city Y' kind of agreement. In general, railway boards were quite willing to betray their friends and change their alliances if it was to their advantage.

In both Britain and the USA one drawback of free-enterprise railway-building, an excess of lines running parallel to each other, was sometimes alleviated by the system of 'running powers' (called 'trackage rights' in the USA). Running powers were confirmed, or imposed, by the legislature at the request of one or more companies, and enabled the trains of one company to run over the tracks of another. They were especially useful in urban areas, where too many tracks were particularly undesirable. But they were a frequent source of discord among companies.

The most notable product of early railway amalgamations was the London & North Western Railway. This became the leading element of the West Coast

Route from London to Glasgow and Aberdeen. It included two of Britain's oldest lines, the Liverpool and Manchester and the London & Birmingham. With such ancient lineage, the LNWR soon advertized itself as the 'Premier Line', a slogan which it kept until it lost its identity in the Railway Amalgamation of 1923. In its early years the Company was dominated by its chairman, Captain Mark Huish. A former official of the East India Company, Huish introduced (or perhaps merely reinforced) the master-and-coolie relationship between officials and subordinates on the LNWR. In the struggles of company against company his strategies were devious and his tactics bullying; so he usually got what he wanted. But not always, for he sometimes overstepped the limit of public toleration. One of his errors of judgement was his 'common purse' arrangement with his ally the Midland Railway, which went a long way towards a real but concealed union of the two companies; when this was revealed in an anti-monopoly parliament during hearings on another of the LNWR's disputes, the Company was savagely criticized. This incident marked the beginning of the end for the 'Euston Confederacy', an unofficial but very powerful grouping of five large companies under the domination of Huish. This bloc had used its considerable weight to do everything possible to take traffic away from rival companies, and notably from the fledgling Great Northern Railway. When Huish attempted to stop the Great Western Railway reaching towards Cheshire, however, he was outfaced.

It happened that a group of small railway companies serving Shrewsbury decided to ally themselves with the Great Western rather than with the LNWR, which meant that they would admit the GW to the territory they served. Huish tried all kinds of manoeuvres to thwart them, from persuasion through threats to actual violence. This became known as the 'Battle of the Shrewsburys', and one of the high points was the bodily ejection by thugs, employed by the LNWR, of booking clerks of one of the Shrewsbury companies at Chester. But with the GWR behind them the Shrewsbury companies, unlike other smaller companies, saw no need to submit to LNWR bullying, with the eventual result that GWR rolling stock did enter the LNWR strongholds of Chester and Liverpool. Such struggles were not uncommon around the middle of the century, and the LNWR was not the only participant. It was known for one company to block another company's line by placing a locomotive or heavily loaded freight cars on its tracks, and there were occasions when gangs of labourers from rival companies would confront each other. Sometimes a magistrate, with uniformed men in support, would be summoned to read the Riot Act to belligerent workers.

Later, the LNWR obtained some kind of revenge by building a long branch line from its Midlands stronghold into South Wales, a preserve of the Great Western which promised enormous coal traffic. But the main preoccupation of the LNWR was the making of money, pursuing feuds with other companies was merely part of that profit-making endeavour. Its trunk route which joined London with Lancashire through the Midlands and Manchester was heavily used, but the Company was always in search of new sources of traffic. When in 1909 Robert E. Peary of the United States Navy reached the North Pole it was remarked that he no doubt found there an LNWR locomotive and freight car, hopefully awaiting new business.

Huish was succeeded by Richard Moon, a gentleman excessively endowed with the late-Victorian virtues. As strict a disciplinarian as Huish, he

was perhaps more honest, but terrified his subordinates with his demanding coldness. Devoting himself to making money for the Company, he succeeded both as a traffic-booster and as a penny-pincher. He ruled from 1861 to 1891, and one of his favourite economies was the dismissal of officials, especially those whom he considered too mild. It was largely owing to him that when the LNWR reached the 20th century it could claim to be Britain's largest railway; the Great Western had a slightly greater mileage, but the LNWR led in the amount of traffic handled.

Possibly the LNWR penny-pinching tradition explains why the Company painted its locomotives black; not only was black paint cheaper and longer-lasting, it was also easier and therefore cheaper to apply. As it was slower to show dirt, it meant that freight locomotives could be cleaned less often. With passenger locomotives it was different; they were black too, but they were always highly-burnished and presented a fine sight at the head of a passenger train, painted in the Company's distinctive livery of purple-brown lower panels and bluish-white uppers. The Company built its own locomotives at Crewe, perhaps the greatest of the British railway towns. In Moon's time the locomotive stock was entrusted to Francis Webb, another of the strict Victorian breed. A capable

Above: Sir Richard Moon of the LNWR.

engineer, Webb's weakness was his temper and his insistence on dominating his subordinates. He created personal conditions around him which meant that not a hint of criticism would reach his ears. This, among other things, enabled him to indulge undisturbed in several of his obsessions. One of these was the compound locomotive; Webb believed he had solved the problem of designing locomotives which would use their steam twice over. Certainly his compounds did pull trains, with a fine

show of sparks, but the tests which
Webb organized to prove how efficient
they were in reality proved nothing; it is
always possible to get improved results
from poor engines by entrusting them to
a highly-skilled crew, providing the
best possible coal, and attending to
other small details that are ignored in
normal operation. Webb also avoided
the use of coupling rods on some of his
compound locomotives, and it was his
combination of compounding, absence
of rods, and an ingenious valve gear
which resulted in one class of
locomotives which, in certain conditions,
could puff powerfully and move not an
inch as the two sets of driving wheels
spun in different directions.

For years it was evident that Webb
would have to go. On the best
passenger trains it became customary to
provide an extra, older, locomotive to
help the compound locomotive to keep
time. Yet so great was the hold on the
Company of Richard Moon (who
appreciated Webb as a man of his own
kind), that it was only after Moon retired
that Webb could be eased out and the
Company provided with reliable
locomotives for the final two decades of
its existence. It was such locomotives,
rather small and thrashed unmercifully
by their crews, that hauled from the
Euston terminus in London the 2-hour

Above: A 'Midland Compound' locomotive restored in Midland Railway livery.
Above left: An LNWR train taking water from track troughs. An old, non-compound locomotive is helping the train's Webb compound locomotive.
Left: The Caledonian blue livery, as used on No 123, a fast 'single' (the term used to denote a single driving axle), built at Glasgow in 1886.

trains to Birmingham which ran in competition against the Great Western's trains. The best LNWR trains in this century were, however, the 'American Specials'. These had superb accommodation, and ran from London to connect with transatlantic liners at Liverpool; in this case it was not competition, but a corporate pride-in-the-job, which stimulated excellence. But it was the Anglo-Scottish trains, operated by the West Coast partnership of the LNWR and Caledonian railways, which the general public regarded as the LNWR's prime services. The West Coast Route, (now, in electrification days, known as the West Coast Main Line or WCML) was the senior of the three main pre-1914 routes to Scotland. The others were the East Coast Route, in constant competition with the West Coast and led by the Great Northern Railway, and the later Midland route, inspired by the Midland Railway and

compensating for its longer and more difficult route by superior rolling stock and superb scenery.

The Caledonian Railway, the Scottish partner of the West Coast Route, opened its main line from the border at Carlisle to Glasgow in 1848. Engineered by Joseph Locke, who disliked tunnels, it featured the Beattock Bank of nearly ten miles (16km) rising at an average 1 in 75 (1.3 per cent) gradient. Later, the Caledonian reached Edinburgh and Aberdeen, thereby extending the area served by the West Coast Route.

The Caledonian was probably not the most characteristic of the Scottish companies, nor was it quite the biggest; its rival, the North British Railway, had more track. But it is still regarded as the greatest of the Scottish railways. It was a solid, well-engineered railway which made great profit from the industrial traffic of Clydeside, from its docks at Grangemouth, and from its coastal steamships. Its trains were not especially fast, but its haulage of the West Coast trains up Beattock Bank demanded substantial locomotives and skilful crews. Its locomotives were very much in the Scottish tradition, being simple and reliable, with little that was fancy. Its locomotive superintendent John McIntosh designed a handsome

range of locomotives that were among the first in Britain to have really adequate steamraising capacity, thanks to their large boilers. From its earliest days the 'Caley' painted its passenger locomotives blue – light blue at first but changing over the decades to the medium 'Caledonian' blue. This livery, and the sonorous whistles favoured by the Company, gave it a distinction which was much savoured by its clients, and also by its own employees who, perhaps more than others, took a real pride in their railway.

The competing East Coast Route was operated by a consortium of the Great Northern and North Eastern railways in England, and the North British in Scotland. The Great Northern was one of the later big companies and, as a newcomer, had to struggle hard against the opposition of established railways. The fight over its parliamentary bill entailed enormous expense and an overnight session of the parliamentary committee. But by the early 1850s, it was running trains from its new and expensive King's Cross terminus in London up to York, where it made an end-on connection with the North Eastern Railway, which in turn had a main line northwards to join the North British at the border.

The LNW and Midland railways, then in close alliance, were early enemies of the Great Northern. When the latter ran a train into the Midland station in Nottingham (which it was entitled to do by means of an agreement with another railway having running powers there), the GN locomotive was surrounded on all sides by Midland locomotives and, unable to extricate itself, was thereupon captured and locked up in a shed for seven months. But five years later the Midland broke away from the LNWR camp and allied itself with the GN, being allowed by the latter running powers over the GN line to London. Meanwhile the GN by another alliance was enabled to run between London and Manchester, much to the disgust of the LNWR management, whose officials tried to block the line with loaded freight trains, and interfered with GN passengers. When this militancy failed, a classic rate war developed, with the delighted Mancunians being offered trips to London by both companies at fares which soon descended to a mere shilling or two.

Edward Bury was the GN's first locomotive superintendent. He did not last long, but had time to introduce one important economy measure; to save paint he instructed that the passenger vehicles should be varnished only. Thus was born the famous 'teak finish' of the Great Northern, used also by its successor the London and North Eastern Railway. The natural wood exteriors of the East Coast trains, hauled by shining apple green locomotives, presented a fine picture. GN locomotives, too, were distinctive. Bury was succeeded by Sturrock, who brought from Swindon the knowledge of how the outstanding Great Western locomotives were made. Using components of standard design where possible, but steadily increasing the number of driving wheels from two to six and (above all) providing ever-larger fireboxes and boilers, Sturrock's successors on the GNR created a breed of locomotives that would culminate in Nigel Gresley's *Flying Scotsman* and *Mallard*.

The East Coast Route's Scottish component, the North British Railway, had built its line from Edinburgh to Berwick in 1844, and had absorbed the key Edinburgh & Glasgow Railway. A feature of the latter was the Cowlairs Incline, leading down to the passenger terminus of Glasgow Queen St at 1 in 45 (2.2 per cent). Locomotives of departing trains were assisted by a cable worked by stationary engines, the cable being slipped at the summit without stopping. The NBR's route to Aberdeen was intersected by the firths of Forth and

Above: The celebrated *Flying Scotsman*, designed by the Great Northern Railway.

Tay, and what are believed to be the world's first train ferries were built to carry freight cars across these obstacles. Passenger vehicles were not handled in this way, but sent by a roundabout route. In the 1870s the Railway seemed to have poor commercial prospects, but an energetic chairman decided to revive its fortunes by bridging the two firths. The bridge over the Tay, the world's longest, was finished in 1878 and in 1879 collapsed in a high wind, taking a train and 80 souls with it. With remarkable determination, and having learned what a difference such a bridge could make to its traffic prospects, the North British immediately built a second Tay Bridge. Then, in 1890, the Company completed what for decades would be regarded as the world's biggest bridge, across the Forth; henceforth Dundee, Aberdeen and Perth were much closer to Edinburgh over North British than over

Caledonian rails. In this undertaking the NBR had the financial support not only of its two East Coast partners, but also of the Midland Railway, each of the four companies granting the builders of the bridge (that is, the Forth Bridge Company) a perpetual guarantee of interest.

At the turn of the century the NBR became the operator of a new line, the West Highland Railway. This was built by a separate company with, unusually for Britain, the financial help of the Treasury; but it was virtually part of the NBR. Passing across Rannoch Moor, with a great horseshoe bend on viaducts at Bridge of Orchy, and breaking through the mountains to reach the west coast of the Highlands at Mallaig, this line remains the most impressively picturesque in Britain. It gave the North British one more feature to suit its chosen image of the most Scottish of the northern railways, an image it presumably pursued because most of its shareholders were English. Its fine Waverley Station could hardly have

Above: Glen Finnan Viaduct on the West Highland line, and Britain's most spectacular railway.
Right: The North British Railway's celebrated bridge over the Firth of Forth.

been closer to the heart of Scotland, nestling between Edinburgh Castle and the capital's main street. It also gave its yellow passenger locomotives names with a Scottish flavour; towards the end they were named after characters from Sir Walter Scott's novels, including such inappropriate names as *The Pirate* and *Cuddie Headrigg*. However, it never went to the expense of fitting nameplates, contenting itself with painting the names on the driving wheel splashers; in this it resembled other Scottish railways, for only the Great North of Scotland had metal nameplates and even those were as short and as thin as possible.

The Forth Bridge reduced the mileage to Aberdeen by 30 miles (48km), although the NBR trains still had to run the final stretch from Kinnabar Junction to Aberdeen over the tracks of

Above: Caledonian Railway enginemen in the 'Race to Aberdeen' of 1895.

their great rival the Caledonian, having running powers over the latter. It was not long before there was an outbreak of 'railway racing' between the East and West coast consortia. Previously, in 1888, there had been the 'Race to Edinburgh', which had been set off when the East Coast admitted third class passengers to its crack 'Flying Scotsman' service from London to Edinburgh. This prompted the West Coast to accelerate their 10 a.m. Scottish expresses, which already carried third class, to match the nine-hour schedule of the East Coast train. In that summer the rivals made successive accelerations to their trains, each trying to outdo the other, until 7¾-hour timings were achieved by both parties. The fastest run was by the East Coast, which despite a compulsory 25-minute lunch break at York ran a train over the course in 7 hours 27 minutes, rather better than their rivals could achieve over a longer and steeper route. Then there came an agreement between the companies by which the fastest day trains were fixed at minimum, 8½-hour timings.

The 'Race to Aberdeen', which was stimulated by the Forth Bridge, occurred in the summer of 1895. The West Coast made a slight acceleration of the night train from London. The East Coast responded by a 20 minute cut in their own schedule, to which the West

Coast replied two weeks later by a further cut of 40 minutes. Acceleration followed acceleration, so that by the end of the summer the 8 p.m. from Euston, which in the spring had reached Aberdeen at 7.40 a.m., reached that granite city at 5.35 a.m.; this was good running over a difficult 540-mile (869-km) route, but it could hardly have been of benefit to the passengers, few of whom could have relished arriving at that unsympathetic hour. On the East Coast, the corresponding 8 p.m. from London arrived at Aberdeen at 5.40 a.m. In reality, both trains were cutting even these reduced schedules, striving for arrivals ahead of schedule. The race was especially dramatic because the trains used the same tracks for the final 38 miles (61km); whichever arrived first at Kinnaber Junction could not be overtaken. The climax came when a somewhat lightened (105-ton) East Coast train arrived in Aberdeen at 4.40 a.m., despite five intermediate stops. The following night the West Coast team, with an even lighter train (70 tons) clattered over their 540 miles at an average speed of 63mph (101km/h), with three intermediate stops. By this time the respective managements, which never acknowledged that anything so undignified as a 'race' was in progress, evidently decided that enough was enough. Great risks had been taken and it is surprising that curves taken at excessive speeds had not derailed any of the trains, although a sober eye-witness did say that he had

seen one locomotive careering round a curve with its offside wheels lifted a few inches above the rail.

Although the Great Northern was the most battle-scarred and most active of the East Coast partners, it was the North Eastern Railway which, in the end, would be regarded as the senior partner. The NER was notable among English companies in that it was both a purely regional railway, with no London ambitions, while at the same time it enjoyed a territorial monopoly of its region (Durham and much of Yorkshire and Northumberland). Contrary to the ideology of the time, the absence of competition did not mean poor service. Usually the reverse was the case; although the NER's local passenger services were mediocre, its main passenger trains, especially the main East Coast Route trains passing over its flat and straight main line between York and Darlington, were very fast. Like its partner the North British, it bridged several water barriers. Its magnificent Royal Border Bridge across the tidal waters of the River Tweed was opened by Queen Victoria in 1850, the same year as another great construction, the High Level Bridge at Newcastle.

Like many railways, the NER varied its livery from decade to decade. Perhaps its finest period, aesthetically, was around the turn of the century, when its passenger trains were painted crimson and its locomotives light green with black and white lining and gold lettering. Its locomotives were typified by sturdiness above all else, but in the 1895 'Race to Aberdeen' an NER 4-4-0, No. 1620, ran from Newcastle to Edinburgh (125 miles or 201km) in 113 minutes. Most of the NER's income came from coal and heavy industry, which were served not only by its rails but by its docks at Hull. It was a pioneer in the use of large capacity (by British standards) coal cars – 20-ton capacity in 1902, 40-ton later. In its last years it also pioneered overhead electrification, converting a short stretch of heavily-used coal line and building electric locomotives. It also ventured into automatic signalling, using compressed gas cylinders to power its signals. Its monopoly was achieved by absorbing all possible competitors; the old Stockton & Darlington Railway was one of its components. Its most serious threat was the Hull & Barnsley Railway, one of the last mainline railways to be built (and also one of the first to be almost totally abandoned). This line was sponsored by Hull malcontents, who believed the NER was serving other, rival, north-eastern ports too well, to the detriment of Hull's own trade. They

Left: On the Lancashire & Yorkshire Railway during its last years; a new large-boiler locomotive designed by George Hughes takes water at speed.
Below: Each railway company had its own characteristic uniforms for those members of the staff in contact with the public. This is a British passenger train guard in Victorian times, holding his regulation railway-issue timepiece.

therefore built their line to capture some of the NER's most lucrative traffic, the coal from Barnsley. But the H & B was never a success, being superfluous, but successive attempts to merge it with the NER failed, usually because of the opposition of Hull commercial interests. It was only on the eve of the great Railway Amalgamation of 1923 that the North Eastern finally swallowed up its rival.

West of the NER territory lay another regional railway, in some ways similar although rather less of a monopoly and with little direct interest in the Anglo-Scottish competition. This was the Lancashire and Yorkshire Railway, a railway which at the end of its life in 1921 was one of the outstandingly well-managed English companies, but which in Victorian times had been one of the shabbiest. It had started as the first railway across the Pennines, calling itself the Manchester and Leeds Railway. At this time, around the middle of the century, the Company was among the smartest. Like most railways of that time, it painted its locomotives dark green, but its passenger vehicles, with dark green lower panels, black uppers, and bright red lining, were enlivened by the scarlet uniforms of the railway guards who were perched high up outside the train in the stage-coach style then common on British railways.

The Lancashire and Yorkshire was the main protagonist in the 'Clifton Incident', which gave the anti-railway press such a great opportunity to scorn the activities, if not the morals, of the railway companies. Like so many incidents, the cause of the friction was running powers. Between Clifton Junction and Manchester the L & Y's main line also carried trains of the rival East Lancashire Railway, by virtue of the latter's running powers. East Lancashire trains stopped at Clifton, where L & Y inspectors went aboard to collect the tickets and to count the passengers, the toll paid by the ELR to the L & Y being based on the number of passengers carried by the former over the tracks of the latter. This arrangement worked reasonably well until the ELR decided to run a faster train that would not stop at Clifton. The L & Y refused this request, on the grounds that it could not trust the ELR to give a faithful declaration of the passenger totals. The ELR duly advertized its new service regardless. On the inaugural day the new train was brought to a halt at Clifton by the L & Y signals and the inspectors boarded, only to be told by irritable passengers that their tickets had already been collected by the ELR inspectors. The train then attempted to proceed towards its destination of Manchester, but after a few score yards came to a halt before a huge mass of timber secured across the track by iron bars driven deep into the ground. Behind this obstruction an L & Y locomotive and train waited on the same track as reinforcement. Anticipating trouble, the ELR had already amassed a force of its workers, who soon demolished the obstruction, leaving the opposing trains face to face. The rival locomotives advanced and a pushing tournament ensued. Neither side seemed able to win this, even after an extra L & Y locomotive had been summoned. Meanwhile, presumably to win a better bargaining position, the ELR forces blocked the other track with a stationary train of stone, with all its brakes pinned down. By midday, when some sort of negotiated settlement was reached, eight trainloads of infuriated passengers were held up by this comedy.

However, a decade later the East Lancashire had been absorbed by the L & Y and the latter, through other amalgamations, was dominant in the industrial areas of Lancashire, while having lines in Yorkshire which stretched as far as the East Coast at Goole. But in the 1870s it was one of Britain's worst railways. Its decrepit locomotive works in Manchester were so disorganized that a spare boiler was successfully burgled, while the locomotive stock was in a state of unrelenting decay; in 1873 these works caught fire, and 26 locomotives were consumed in the flames, as well as about 100 passenger vehicles. L & Y trains were slow and passengers to Bradford, one of the main traffic centres, feared that they would be choked in the sulphurous fumes of the steeply graded tunnels leading to the station.

But by 1914 the L & Y had passed through a renaissance. A new and cleverly designed works at Horwich built and repaired locomotives. The latter were of reliable design, thanks to the Railway's import from India of a sound locomotive superintendent. A subsequent locomotive superintendent, John Aspinall, designed some remarkable 4-4-2 locomotives with, unusually for Britain, really large boilers and driving wheels of over 7ft (2,133mm) diameter; these new locomotives helped to accelerate the passenger services, in company with tank locomotives that were unusual in being fitted to take water from water troughs. Aspinall was one of the few mechanical engineers to rise further and become general manager. Under his leadership the L & Y began to electrify its Liverpool-Southport commuter line in 1904, and on the eve of World War I introduced the first British all-steel mainline train (advertized as the 'fireproof train', after a disastrous train fire on the Midland Railway in 1913). When, on the eve of the general railway amalgamation, the L & Y consented to lose its formal identity by merging with the LNWR it was strong enough to do so on its own terms; its locomotive superintendent, George Hughes, one of the few really scientific British locomotive designers, subsequently set about rejuvenating Crewe's locomotive policies with ideas brought from Horwich.

A much smaller northern local railway, possessing little more than a hundred miles of route, was the Furness Railway. This served Cumbria and the Lake District so its red locomotives and blue-and-white trains were known to a wider audience. As it served the industrial city of Barrow, too, it had

Above: Crest of the LMS Railway, of which the Midland and LNWR were the main constituents.

enough traffic to enable it to maintain its independence.

A third route from London to Scotland was that initiated by the Midland Railway. Although this company began as a purely regional enterprise it ended as a national railway serving places as far afield as Bristol, London, the North, and even South Wales. At Bromsgrove, on the former Birmingham & Gloucester Railway, it had Britain's most arduous climb, the 2-mile (3-km) Lickey Incline at 1 in 37 (2.7 per cent). For a time, the Midland was part of Britain's first but short-lived Anglo-Scottish route, which used its line from near Birmingham to York; but with the opening of the West Coast Route the Midland had lost this traffic.

To reach London the Midland at first obtained running powers over the Great Northern main line southwards from Hitchin. The GNR was quite glad to offer a share of its line, for in so doing it detached the Midland from its long alliance with the London & North Western. However, the GN line between London and Hitchin soon became overcrowded, and at one period the GN management had to restrict Midland

freight traffic. This encouraged the latter to build its own London extension, and its grandiose terminus at St Pancras. Despite the money spent on this extension, the MR soon made its bid for the Scottish traffic by building the difficult Settle & Carlisle line across the northern fells from Leeds to link with the Glasgow & South Western Railway at Carlisle. With its summit at Ais Gill, 22 miles (35km) of track at 1 in 100 (1 per cent), nineteen viaducts, and three miles (5km) of tunnel, this was one of the most difficult of British lines, both to build and to operate. Many lives were lost during construction, but when finished it was, and remains, a main line of great scenic attraction. For its debut the MR introduced Pullman coaches; these were third class vehicles with upholstered seats, the first twelve-wheelers to run on British railways. Its two partners (the Glasgow & South Western provided the Glasgow connection but the North British was used for the Edinburgh service) joined in providing other superior vehicles for the new Anglo-Scottish trains.

Although much of the Midland's revenue came from its coal traffic from Nottinghamshire to London (to accommodate which it added two freight-only tracks to its existing

double-track main line from London) and its services on the south-west to north-east axis (Bristol-Birmingham-Yorkshire) were also of great importance, it tended to lavish the most care on its newer Anglo-Scottish service. But the MR, having very few routes that were not threatened by competitors, could never relax and was always ready to innovate. It was the Midland which took the long step forward of abolishing, in effect, the traditional third class. What it did was to re-label second class as third, and cease offering second class. This was a coup which brought great joy to the travelling public, who on the MR obtained second class standards for the price of a third class ticket, but great dismay to the other companies which all, sooner or later, had to follow the MR example. In the following century the nationalized British Railways renamed third class as second, bringing the MR's initiative to a logical conclusion. The tradition of soft upholstered seats for the lower class was firmly established by 1914, and still means that British standards of second class comfort are higher than

Left: Crest of the Birmingham & Derby Junction Railway, soon to become part of the Midland Railway.
Below: Inside a British first class compartment in the mid Nineteenth century.

those of other west European railways. Externally, too, the MR was distinctive, painting its passenger locomotives and trains a rich maroon colour with black and yellow lining and gold lettering. It was for long a user of the 'single' (one pair of driving wheels) locomotive, whose utility it prolonged by developing steam-sanding equipment to give its wheels extra adhesion on the rails; this steam sander soon became standard equipment on other railways' locomotives. In its last decades the MR produced the most successful range of compound locomotives to run on British railways while, in its early days, it had pioneered the brick-arch firebox, enabling coal to be burned instead of coke.

Among the southern railways, the Great Western was the dominant company. Although it went through a difficult period in the 1860s, by the 20th century it had regained its position as a standard-setter. It was an excellent railway, although not always quite as excellent as it claimed. Its local services were mediocre and its clients were often treated with exasperating condescension; travelling on the Great Western was like staying at the grandest of grand hotels. In the late 19th century its main rival was the London and South Western Railway, which had a much shorter route from London to Devon. Competitive schedules were at their sharpest in the 'Ocean Mail' services which met transatlantic liners at Plymouth. It was when working one of these trains in 1904 that the GWR *City of Truro* reached its reputed 102mph (164km/h). The same year a competing LSWR 'Ocean Mail', intent on beating the GWR competition, flew off the rails on the curve at Salisbury, with heavy loss of life. This coincided with the opening of one of the TWR's cut-off routes, shortening its run to Plymouth, and these two circumstances put an end to the racing between the two companies. Soon there was a 'working agreement', a quite common arrangement by which competing companies arranged non-competitive schedules and split the revenue in an agreed proportion.

The GWR built several cut-offs, perhaps conscious of its nickname the 'Great Way Round'. The earliest and most expensive was the Severn Tunnel, which considerably shortened the London to South Wales journey. Here it was not a question of competition, because there never was any competition on that route; rather it was a matter of reducing operating costs. The passengers, moreover, had a quicker trip, and could savour the sulphurous

Above: The arms of London and Bristol combined to form the GWR crest.

pleasure of pounding through the world's longest underwater tunnel. Another cut-off shortened the London to Birmingham route to 110 miles (177km), enabling the GWR to compete successfully against the LNWR for the passenger traffic.

In the 20th century Great Western locomotives gave the Company extra distinction, for not only did they look quite different from those of any other railway, but they were technically far in advance, enabling the GWR to operate fast and heavy trains at low cost. In appearance they combined the gauntness of the American locomotive with the smooth lines of the British. Painted in Brunswick green, with polished brass fittings (including large name and number plates), and with copper-capped chimneys, they made a fine sight at the head of trains painted in the GWR livery of chocolate lower panels and cream uppers. Moreover,

burning the renowned Welsh steam coal, they showed hardly a trace of smoke at their chimneys.

Of the railways originating south of the Thames, the GWR's great rival, the London & South Western, was the most substantial. Indeed, in the 1840s the LSWR and the GWR had been regarded as Britain's two leading companies. The LSWR was originally the London & Southampton Railway. It soon built a branch to Gosport in order to serve Portsmouth. It had also planned to reach Bath, but was forestalled by the GWR. Engineered by Locke, its main line bore all the characteristics of that engineer: an avoidance of tunnels, an up-and-over philosophy which produced long sections of straight track, deep cuttings and high embankments. In the 1840s it seemed to be the only standard gauge company that could approach the broad-gauge GWR in its train speeds. Perhaps this was because its locomotive department was in the charge of John Gooch, brother of Daniel Gooch who was locomotive superintendent of the

GWR. As early as 1846 the LSWR operated a special train over the 78 miles (125km) from Southampton to London at an average speed of 50mph (81km/h).

Soon, the LSWR reached Exeter and, by calculated mergers with existing companies, took its main line around the north of Dartmoor to reach another GWR preserve, Plymouth and Cornwall. For a couple of miles at Exeter the LSWR trains used running powers over the Great Western main line, and at periods when competition was hottest the local GWR staff could always be relied on to find a good operating reason to delay the LSWR trains.

Over the years the LSWR gained the reputation of a rather unexciting but individualistic and reliable carrier. Its passenger coaches were dark brown, with salmon-pink upper panels, and looked a fine sight behind the pale green locomotives with their chocolate, black and white lining. In reality the Company was more forward-looking than was realized. It virtually created the port of Southampton, and at one time it provided the best link, via Southampton and Le Havre, between London and Paris. Indeed the railway between Paris and Le Havre owed much to the LSWR; when the French public failed to invest enough capital to launch the main line to Le Havre the banker Lafitte appealed, in person, to the board of the LSWR and was provided not only with the needed capital but also with a large contingent of British labour including, finally, British locomotive men and the British locomotive designer William Buddicom. In its final years the Company despatched a delegation to American railroads, after which it introduced American-style automatic signalling, and heavy 100lb rails. Its electrification of suburban services from its Waterloo terminus in London used the third-rail system, which was later adopted as standard by the new Southern Railway, into which the LSWR was incorporated in 1923.

A neighbour of the LSWR and, before a working agreement was reached, a serious competitor for the Portsmouth traffic, was the London, Brighton, and South Coast Railway. This is an example of a railway which provided an undistinguished service yet succeeded in winning public esteem by being both different and aesthetically pleasing. Its initial main line, connecting London and Brighton, was finished in 1841, passing through the scenic South Downs and culminating in the magnificent curved viaduct carrying the line high over the rooftops of Brighton. Apart from its extension to Portsmouth, it came to serve the region south of London, becoming primarily a passenger-carrying railway with relatively short-distance service. In the 20th century its suburban and outer-suburban traffic was so heavy that it had to quadruple the London end of its main line. Also, in 1909 it electrified an inner-suburban line to meet competition from London electric tramway companies. However, although this electrification was later extended the LBSCR system of overhead conductor wire did not long survive the merging of the Company into the Southern Railway. Steam traction in any case predominated to the end. The so-called 'improved engine green' (actually yellow) livery of the locomotives was one of those features which endeared the line to its public. Another was its installation of steam heating in its suburban trains, the first railway in Britain to do so. Being a passenger line of short distances, it possessed hardly any freight locomotives, and made great use of tank locomotives, including some very large (by British standards) 4-6-4 tanks for fast trains. Its 'Southern Belle' service between London and Brighton provided Pullman cars for third class passengers.

Uncomfortably constricted by the LSWR to the west, the LBSCR was equally constrained in the east by the South Eastern Railway. At the time when the first lines of the LBSCR and SER were built, Parliament was wise enough to stipulate that they should use the tracks of the older London & Greenwich Railway into the capital. The latter, a short line built on a high brick viaduct over the suburbs, seemed to parliamentarians quite adequate, and there was an understandable dislike of railways cutting their way into cities. Moreover, after the Greenwich rails the SER and LBSCR trains were to share a new line for several miles. This was a sure recipe for squabbles, and the two companies quarrelled almost immediately. The SER was destined to be in conflict for most of its life, for it was soon challenged by the London, Chatham & Dover Railway, which built a line to Canterbury and Dover much shorter than that of the SER. And so in this Kentish corner of England there arose an extreme case of commercial competition, with the SER and LCDR each attempting to damage the other and to gain enough traffic to make a profit. Almost every town of any size was soon served by a station of each company, with train services designed to capture as much traffic as possible from the other. While the SER, sharing the Victoria terminus with the LBSC, had no real need for more stations in London, both the LCDR and the SER built new stations there, so that the capital is still littered with them. At Dover, competing boat trains waited side by side on the quay for the ferries from France, and railway staff would endeavour to hustle as many passengers as possible on to their own company's train. On one occasion the ferry arrived

Below: Peace at last: the crest resulting from the SER and LCDR alliance in 1899.

33

with just one passenger, and blows were exchanged as the companies' servants struggled for his custom. And yet, with all this cut-throat competition, the public received a rather poor service. Each company so impoverished itself in trying to outdo the other on a few glamorous services that there were few resources left to improve the ordinary services. In the end the two rivals abandoned the competitive system and joined in a full-scale working agreement, with the formation of a management committee under which the railways, nominally independent, were joined under the title of South Eastern & Chatham Railway and split the profits, 41 per cent of the latter going to the LCDR.

The last main line to reach London did so as late as 1898. This was the Great Central Railway, previously operating under the name of Manchester, Sheffield and Leeds Railway but renamed to accord with its new ambitions. The M S & L had its origins in a railway built through the Pennines to link Manchester with Sheffield. It was the possessor of the famous Woodhead Tunnel, whose construction had been difficult, whose labourers had split into warring English and Irish factions, and which when opened treated passengers (and locomotive men even more) to thick suffocating fumes produced by locomotives climbing steeply through its narrow bore. To reach London the Railway joined with the Metropolitan Railway; the latter was a London underground line which had also become ambitious and sprouted a 'main line' into London's northern suburbs and countryside. Great Central trains coming from the north over the new GCR extension through Leicester and Rugby used the Metropolitan's track until they diverged to the Company's

brand new London terminus at Marylebone. Being a newcomer, and opposed by the existing north to south railways (LNWR, Midland, and GNR), the Great Central had to try hard, and its trains were sumptuously furnished and tightly scheduled. Indeed the locomotive work of the GCR before 1914 was probably surpassed only on the Great Western, and it was a GCR locomotive design which was chosen as Britain's freight locomotive for overseas service in World War I. But despite the magnificence of the venture, another railway to London was not really needed and it is not surprising that the GCR London extension was the first main line to be closed during the economy drive of the 1960s.

Most of the Great Central's London extension passed through agricultural areas which even now have been little developed. But the GCR's older lines tapped enough coal and industrial territory to keep the Company out of bankruptcy, even though dividends were small. Several of Britain's railways did not have this advantage, being lines which nowadays would be described as developmental, intended to open up new regions rather than to make a profit. A railway which was almost in this category, but not quite, was the Great Eastern, serving the cathedral towns and arable acres of East Anglia. But for the fact that it started from London, where it operated the country's densest suburban service out of its Liverpool Street terminus, this Company would have been as impecunious as some of the Highland and Irish lines. It had its beginnings in the Eastern Counties Railway, which opened from London to Colchester in the mid-1840s. The Eastern Counties had a poor reputation. It started badly, adopting the five foot gauge for no good reason and

changing to standard gauge almost immediately, and it had unnecessarily steep gradients out of London. But after a series of mergers had transformed it into the Great Eastern Railway its reputation improved. It was a pioneer in oil-burning locomotives; its boat train to Harwich (connecting with vessels for the Netherlands) required smart work and its later locomotives, painted a handsome blue, were well-designed and well-built in its workshops in East London.

The Scottish highlands was a region that would never produce great dividends for railway companies, but nevertheless the railway did come. Initially, it was Aberdeen and Inverness which sought a link. The Aberdonians launched the Great North of Scotland Railway which, however, never managed to reach Inverness. It did manage to get as far as Elgin, where it connected with another line, but its service was so poor that the Inverness citizens supported a new enterprise, the Highland Railway. The latter eventually comprised a single track main line from Perth to Inverness and then to the very top of Scotland at Thurso and Wick. It was a desolate line, never making enough money to properly equip itself. Its moment of glory was World War I, when it was the link with the Grand Fleet at Scapa Flow. The 'Jellicoe Specials', daily trains carrying sailors from London to the fleet, were worked expeditiously, but so ill-equipped was the Company that locomotives had to be borrowed from the English railways. The HR's relationship with the GNSR was never good. The latter had a sparse network around Aberdeen, and was the operator of the 'royal' Deeside line, serving Queen Victoria's residence at Balmoral. Like mid-century American railroads, it hauled both passenger and freight trains with 4-4-0 type locomotives. Where the GNSR and HR lines met it became almost a tradition for both companies to schedule their trains to depart just before the arrival of the 'connecting' train of the other company.

Wales, like Scotland, had a large expanse of mountainous and unproductive terrain joined to an industrial area. The latter was the South Wales coal basin. The Great Western tapped this with its main line from London to Newport, Cardiff, Swansea and Fishguard, while up the valleys toiled the coal trains of the small South

Left: Smartly timed and smartly turned out, the Great Central Railway's 'Sheffield Luncheon Car Express' gathers speed outside London on the eve of World War I.

Wales companies, notably those of the Taff Vale, Rhymney, and Barry railways. All these coal lines were great users of the tank locomotive, especially the 0-6-2 tank, for their relatively short runs over the winding rails of the valleys. These proletarian lines, with their black begrimed locomotives, contrasted sharply with the impecunious but dignified Cambrian Railway which served Central Wales. Nothing was more characteristic of the Cambrian's threadbare respectability than its locomotive liveries, for it painted its locomotives, both passenger and freight, black, but embellished each of them with a fine representation of the Prince of Wales's feathers. The Cambrian had its main line from Whitchurch through Oswestry and Welshpool to Machynlleth, where it divided to serve (and develop as seaside resorts) Aberystwyth in the south and the coastal towns of the north. The Cambrian coast line up to Barmouth was, and is, a spectacular piece of engineering, being in many places hacked out of the cliffs; on two occasions a train has fallen off this line and smashed on the rocks far below. Further north, the Great Western had a quiet line from Wrexham westwards to Dolgelley, while along the northern coast the LNWR had its main line to Holyhead and Ireland. The route of the 'Irish Mail', the latter had the world's first water troughs laid near Conway; these were invented by the LNWR after the British Post Office had imposed fast schedules for the Irish mail trains, making it necessary for locomotives to pick up their water without stopping.

The LNWR interest in Ireland did not end at the quayside at Holyhead. From that harbour it ran its own steamers across to Dublin and at North Wall in the Irish capital had its own freight station. Not only this, but it was also owner of the Dundalk, Newry and Greenore Railway, for which Crewe supplied LNWR locomotives and rolling stock, modified to work on the Irish 5ft 3in (1,600mm) gauge. The Midland Railway also had its Irish interests. From 1904 it had a steamer service from its Heysham Harbour in Lancashire to Belfast, and its Northern Counties Committee had over 250 miles (402km) of railway in Ireland, including the 5ft 3in (1,600mm) gauge Belfast-Londonderry line. Ireland's first railway was the short Dublin & Kingstown, built to standard gauge in 1834. In 1839 another gauge, 6ft 2in (1,880mm), appeared with the Ulster Railway from Belfast to Armagh. Later, however, the 5ft 3in (1,600mm) gauge became the Irish standard, although many lines, especially in the less populated areas, were narrow gauge, usually 3ft (914mm). Irish railways were never prosperous, and the narrow gauge lines in particular had that peculiar attraction which comes from railways struggling against all the odds to remain in existence despite the apparent hopelessness of finding enough traffic to cover costs. Ireland had very few railways that could be described as mainline. The Great Southern & Western's Dublin to Cork line was perhaps the most notable route, followed by the Belfast-Dublin line of the Great Northern of Ireland, the Dublin-Wexford line of the Dublin and South Eastern, and the Belfast-Londonderry and Belfast-Larne lines of the Northern Counties Committee.

It was not only British railways that had their offices in London. Many overseas railways were British-owned, and even in the 1970s there were a handful which still held their annual meeting of shareholders in London. Virtually a second British railway system was created in India. There were several large companies sharing this network, but government control was quite close and it was a planned network rather than a network created by uncontrolled private enterprise; in places there was competition, but in general the government ensured that railways were evenly distributed and that no two places were connected by more than one railway. But despite the lessons of the 'Battle of the Gauges' in Britain, the British did leave India the legacy of a four-gauge system; most lines were broad gauge (5ft 6in or 1,676mm) or metre gauge, but there were also 2ft 6in (760mm) and 2ft (610mm) gauges. The broad gauge had been intended as the standard, but when the need for railways increased beyond the amount of money available it was decided to introduce the cheaper metre gauge. In Australia, too, the British left a gauge problem, but this was more a result of muddle and of local state politics than a fault of the London authorities, which at least tried to set a standard gauge. The adoption by different states of different gauges only became a hindrance when the various systems expanded towards the state frontiers, where break-of-gauge interchange stations had to be established. Although the construction of the Trans Australian Railway, linking the eastern states with Western Australia,

Below: British-built locomotives await their duties at Sydney, New South Wales.

confirmed that 4ft 8½in (1,435mm) was the government's preference, the conversion of the 5ft 3in (1,600mm) lines of Victoria and South Australia, and the 3ft 6in (1,067mm) lines of Western Australia to standard gauge has been minimal, permitting standard gauge through traffic on only a handful of routes, while Tasmania and Queensland had little intention of converting their 3ft 6in (1,067mm) gauge systems to standard gauge.

The Indian Railway companies, and to a lesser extent those of Australia and other parts of the British Empire, were the principal markets for the British locomotive building industry. Although for a few years in the 1830s British builders had a virtual monopoly of locomotive exports this situation did not last. German and American locomotive builders, in particular, soon began to compete with the British. The latter had the peculiar disadvantage that they did not have a prosperous home market on which to base their export drive. The big British railway companies, unlike the American and continental, built their own locomotives in their own workshops to their own design, which meant that for British locomotive builders the export trade was by far the main business, home orders being received only when the railway companies needed more locomotives than they could build themselves. Export locomotives, apart from details like lamps, cabs, and cowcatchers, were very British in design, and indeed by the 1970s India had become the best country to see traditional British locomotives at work. From time to time the colonial governments did import non-British locomotives, probably to remind the British builders that their virtual monopoly of the trade was not to be taken for granted. Moreover, more and more overseas railways or nations began to build their own locomotives. Somewhat exceptional among these was the Canadian Pacific Railway which, although a British company with its headquarters in London, from the start steadfastly refrained from buying British locomotives, preferring American designs, and then progressed to building its own.

Nevertheless, the Canadian Pacific was the most British of the North American railways, being very much an Empire project designed to secure the integrity of a coast-to-coast Canada. In general, the British played a small role in the USA, although many of the 19th

Left: The Canadian Pacific Railway, ever confident, advertizes a new, slower, route to the west.

century railroad companies relied heavily on British capital; the famous locomotive *Gowan and Marx* was named in honour of the London bankers who had financed its owner, the Philadelphia and Reading Railroad. The USA resembled Britain in that the railway network was not planned, the choice of routes being left to the interplay of conflicting commercial interests. The result was that in the USA railways were built fast, but were not always located rationally. For example, although the several railways connecting New York with Chicago touched on different towns en route it is difficult to justify their number; indeed, dividing the traffic in this way meant that not one of the companies could really earn enough revenue to provide the further investment needed for the best possible service. One large railroad, the Nickel Plate Railroad, was built simply by one group of interests in order to threaten another, and there were many lesser but similar incidents. Financial skulduggery, which was only a minor feature of the British railway age, was a normal occurrence among American railroads. Stock manipulations in which, typically, railroad managements artificially depressed the value of their companies' shares, perhaps by spreading depressing rumours, and then buying up the stock themselves, were quite frequent. Millions of dollars were thereby taken from investors and placed in the pockets of the millionaire railroad kings. Cornelius Vanderbilt, who more or less created the New York Central Railroad, was perhaps the most notorious of these 'robber barons', though not quite the most unscrupulous of them. He died an honoured multi-millionaire. Despite his millions, he had initiated the practice of painting locomotives black, as an economy measure, and this example was followed elsewhere as American companies abandoned their yellow, red or green liveries in favour of something cheaper. One of Vanderbilt's more endearing coups was enacted when the rival Erie Railroad advertized a cut-price (and below cost) reduction of freight rates on live cattle between Chicago and New York; Vanderbilt ordered his agents to purchase all available cattle and to despatch them by the Erie RR.

But the US railways were built expeditiously. It was not usually necessary to adopt the continental European and Indian governments' device of guaranteeing the dividends on capital invested in railways, in order to coax money out of the public. However, there was the land-grant device, by which long-distance railways traversing

virgin territory were offered a certain extent of free land per mile of track as an inducement. This did enrich many lines, including the transcontinentals. Much of the land was offered by the railroad to incoming immigrants, thereby populating the continent and providing an economic base for railway operations. Some of the land was retained by the railroads and there are several which today have cause to be grateful for this, coal and oil having

Above: A British-built 0-6-0 still at work in Pakistan.

been found on their vast landholdings.

Elsewhere in the world governments usually insisted on planning their railway networks. Strict government intervention was responsible for the star-shaped form of the French main lines, radiating from Paris; this meant that very few cities apart from Paris had more than one railway, which in turn

meant that the capital available for railway building was spent more wisely than in Britain and America. It also meant that the shape of French economic development has been determined by a handful of politicians, and the French railway network did in fact make Paris even more the centre of the country, a feature which many found undesirable and which had some serious military implications. In Germany there was less centralization because the early railways were constructed by the individual states, and as their main aim was to improve commercial prospects the lines tended to form a rational network when they joined up with each other. Prussia's dominance did make Berlin the biggest of the German railway centres, but it never resembled Paris in this respect. In both France and Germany the small companies, whether state or private, soon merged to form large organizations. The first to be thus formed was the Northern Railway (Nord) in France in the 1840s. This proved to be a very successful and profitable line, but not for long was it the biggest. The Paris-Lyons-Mediterranean Railway (PLM), with its trunk route from Paris through Lyons to Marseilles, soon became preeminent, although in locomotive matters and in subsequent electrification it was the Paris-Orleans Railway (PO), serving south-western France as well as the centre, which took a lead. In Germany, because of the political and territorial predominance of Prussia, it was the Prussian Royal State Railways which soon predominated. Many of the Prussian lines were built for strategic reasons, towards the eastern and western frontiers and along those frontiers. When war broke out with France in 1870 the Prussian railways were well prepared with emergency timetables and the German troops were in position on the frontier before the French. However, when the Prussians advanced it was found that in France the Prussian locomotives damaged their chimneys and cabs against lineside structures; henceforth, and even after the merging of the state railways into the *Deutsche Reichsbahn* after World War I, German locomotives were designed with detachable chimney tops and smallish cabs. The gibe that in Germany the railways operated locomotives designed to run on other countries' lines was founded on fact.

Left: The last years of American steam: a Milwaukee, St Paul & Pacific Railroad 4-6-2 leaves Chicago hauling a local train in 1952.

The Pursuit of Excellence

In Britain, Continental Europe, and North America 1914 may be regarded as the end of a great railway era. In the decades preceding World War I the railways, while keeping their monopoly of land transport, nevertheless greatly improved their services. Trains became faster, safer, and more reliable, while not becoming more expensive to their users. Passenger schedules were cut but at the same time trains became heavier due to the provision of more comfortable accommodation for all classes. The practice of running named trains grew, trains like the Great Northern's 'Flying Scotsman', the LNWR's 'Irish Mail', the Pennsylvania Railroad's 'Broadway Limited', as well as such great international trains as the 'Orient Express'. Such trains were regarded as the flagships of the companies operating them, showing just what the railways could do and also providing a foretaste of the high standard which sooner or later would spread downwards to the less celebrated trains.

In Britain more than anywhere else in the world train schedules were a matter of great public interest. Partly this was because so many pairs of cities were linked by more than one railway, and competitive scheduling was regarded as almost a sporting spectacle by the newspaper-reading public. Partly it was because many Britons had fallen into the habit of regarding time as money; much of the commercial middle class felt that time spent travelling was quite unproductive, and therefore a reduction of five minutes in the train time between two places might be regarded as an important gain. In other countries a different philosophy prevailed, although in Germany, the Netherlands, and the USA, businessmen began to resemble the British in their attitude. For the general public, a few minutes here or there was of little importance, what really mattered was the cheapness of the fare and the degree of comfort provided by the railway companies; here, too, the railways were able to gratify their clients.

After 1850 it was the Great Western and Great Northern railways which were the most notable for their fast passenger trains. In the 1870s the GWR 'Flying Dutchman' from London to the West of England was scheduled over the 77 miles (123km) from London to Swindon at 53mph (85km/h); this stretch of almost level track was destined to be the Great Western's racing ground, and

Left: The era of the great international trains; a poster of the International Sleeping Car Company.

in later decades would witness the passage of such crack trains as the 'Cheltenham Flyer' and, eventually, the High Speed Train. In the 1870s the GWR was notable, too, in that it endeavoured to accelerate the general run of its trains to speeds approaching those of its crack services. On the Great Northern, Sturrock's locomotives, built on Great Western principles, were also achieving some smart timings. Despite some miles of climbing at 1 in 105 (0.9 per cent) out of the King's Cross terminus, the London to Hitchin timing was brought down to 38 minutes for the 32 miles in the late 1850s. By the 1870s the main train to Scotland, the 10 a.m. 'Flying Scotsman' from King's Cross, took only $9\frac{1}{2}$ hours to Edinburgh, while the London to Leeds service averaged 50mph (80km/h). Other railways were less sprightly, although the London & North Western in 1862 ran a very fast special train with vital despatches from the USA concerning the 'Trent Case' (an incident which might have led to an Anglo-American war); this train ran from the quay at Holyhead to London in record time, with the 133 miles (214km) between Stafford and London being run non-stop by a locomotive with a special tender, which covered its first 50 miles (80km) in 46 minutes. On the London & South Western Railway there were smart schedules on the Exeter line, a hilly length which demanded superb

Below: The Great Western Railway's 'Flying Dutchman' in the early Twentieth century, hauled by one of the fast 'City' class locomotives.

locomotive work to keep time. But the Railway's Southampton service, where there was no competition, was slow. Among Britain's most mediocre performers were the Lancashire & Yorkshire Railway, whose 'crack' Bradford-Manchester train took 80 minutes to cover 41 miles (66km) and the Great North of Scotland, whose best Aberdeen-Elgin train needed 245 minutes to cover 72 miles (116km).

By the turn of the century the USA and France were beginning to outshine Britain in train speeds. In the USA, especially, some very creditable schedules had been introduced. On the short run from Camden, New Jersey, to Atlantic City, high speed trains hauled by 4-4-2 type locomotives ('Atlantics') covered $55\frac{1}{2}$ miles (89km) in 50 minutes, and these were the world's fastest trains at the end of the 1890s. Longer-distance American trains were also being accelerated. The Illinois Central brought the Chicago-New Orleans timing down to 25 hours, while in 1902 the New York Central and the Pennsylvania railways were operating their rival '20th Century Limited' and 'Pennsylvania Special' on 20-hour schedules between New York and Chicago. Three years later these timings had been cut to 18 hours, bringing the trains into the 50mph (80km/h) class. In France, also, there were several really good trains. From Paris to Bordeaux, for example, the timing for the 362 miles (583km) had been brought down by the Paris-Orleans Railway to 6hrs 54min by 1913; this was well above a 50mph (80km/h) average; and was achieved by the 'Sud

Express', a supplementary-fare train of the International Sleeping Car Company. In Germany a 56mph (90km/h) average speed was achieved the same year by the fastest of the Berlin-Hamburg trains of the Prussian Royal State Railways.

In Britain at the turn of the century there were only five trains scheduled at more than 55mph (88km/h); three of these were short runs on the Caledonian between Forfar and Perth, and two on the Great Northern. However, compared to the USA and the continent Britain excelled in the standards of its ordinary services. While trains like the '20th Century Limited' and 'Sud Express' were supplementary-fare trains for first class passengers, the fastest British trains were open to all at no extra fare, and the run-of-the-mill long-distance train was faster in Britain than similar overseas trains. Moreover, between 1900 and 1914, sometimes regarded as the Golden Age of Britain's railways, there was steady acceleration of train services. The GWR led the way. From 1904 its 'Cornish Riviera Limited' ran non-stop from London to Plymouth and by 1914 covered the 226 miles (364km) at 55mph (88km/h). In that year the Great Western scheduled no fewer than 33 non-stop runs of over 100 miles (161km). However this was exceeded by the LNWR with 41, while the GNR had 22. The fastest schedules were operated over the North Eastern Railway between Darlington and York, where 44 miles (71km) were covered in 43 minutes, and over the Great Central between Leicester and Nottingham ($22\frac{1}{2}$ miles or 36km in 22 minutes); both these

Flying Dutchman G.W.R.
NEAR SLOUGH.

Above: The first British dining car on the Great Northern Railway in 1879.

represented average speeds of 61½mph (99km/h).

The gradual introduction of steel rails and steel tyres, both harder than the previous iron types, lowered train resistance, enabling a given locomotive to haul a heavier load. However, bigger locomotives were still required, because trains became heavier. This increased weight was due not so much to the running of longer trains, but to the increasing weight of vehicles. Up to about 1860 this increase was imperceptible, there being few improvements in rolling stock. The four-wheeler was still standard in Britain and on the Continent, although the Great Northern had begun to favour six-wheelers. The old third class car, quite open to the elements, had disappeared. The 'Gladstone Act', which had made compulsory the running of third class accommodation over every line at fares no more than one penny per mile, had also specified that third class passengers should be decently covered from the elements. But those railways which offered the very cheap fourth class were not obliged to provide closed vehicles for it. There were a few innovations; as early as the 1840s the

Grant Junction had a 'bed carriage' which, although not a true sleeping car, did enable its passengers to stretch themselves out on boards laid between seats. In 1852 the GWR built some long eight-wheelers which, however, did not run on true bogies. Illumination, when provided, was by a few oil lamps suspended from the ceiling, and in the 1850s it was still a common practice to carry luggage on the roof. Perhaps the biggest change was introduced by a private member's amendment to a parliamentary bill, by which it was made compulsory for every train to have at least one vehicle made available for smoking. Hitherto smoking had been prohibited by most railways, because of the peril of train fires.

The later part of the 19th century witnessed many improvements not only in train furnishing, but in such important matters as the provision of toilets, good heating and lighting, and dining and sleeping facilities. At the end of the century most trains still did not provide toilets. The earliest train toilets appear to have been those of Queen Victoria's royal saloon on the South Eastern Railway, but it was long before even first class passengers could avail themselves of this luxury. Train stops were expected to be long and frequent enough for a passenger to do what he

or she needed to do. Often, however, they were not, and there were sometimes bitter and embarrassing scenes when a night train made its first stop in the early morning at a station with insufficient facilities to satisfy pent-up demand. In the third class people were less sophisticated, and either took pots with them or used whatever cover they could find at the lineside. It was not really until the corridor train became common that this problem could be solved. Before then, some railways had ladies-only compartments, with a shared toilet placed between two compartments. The so-called family saloons were also provided with them; the latter style of vehicle was an open car, with inward-facing seats around the sides, and was intended to be reserved by a family or large group.

By 1900 eight-wheelers, running on two bogies, were becoming more numerous, and in 1891 the GWR introduced the first complete train of side-corridor vehicles with the now-familiar gangway connection between them. However, many people, including King Edward VII, disliked corridors; they said there was no privacy with people walking up and down beside the compartments. Vehicles had wooden bodies and usually wooden frames, two circumstances which made them unsafe

TRAIN DE LUXE

Jadis, quand une jol
femme, grande dame
bourgeoise, voyageait
chaise de poste en comp
gnie d'un mari vieux ba
bon, la route était propi
aux amoureuses aventures
Un galant cavalier, comm
par hasard, se trouvait fair
même trajet et parcoura
mêmes étapes aux même
heures. Il dépassait la ber
line, se laissait rejoindre
récoltait chaque fois un re
gard, obtenait un sourir
aux relais, dérobait un bai
ser ou mieux encore à l'hô
tellerie, tandis que le griso
était plongé dans la lectur
du dernier numéro du Mer
cure.

Aujourd'hui... il n'y a de
changé que le décor, le véhi
cule, les costumes des per
sonnages et le titre de la
gazette.

Above: Restaurant and buffet cars varied between companies and countries. This picture is quite representative of the best standards around 1910.
Right: By the Twentieth century the GNR was providing third class dining cars.

in accidents, as they readily smashed or burned. Train fires were especially lethal in the period when gas lighting was superceding oil lamps. The London, Brighton & South Coast Railway was the first to provide successful electric lighting from dynamos run by belts from the axles of the cars themselves.

Train heating was for long regarded as an unnecessary luxury by most companies. After all, the stage coaches had been unheated, and anyone who could survive a winter trip by stagecoach could surely not complain about unheated trains. Foot-warmers filled with hot water were sometimes encountered in first class compartments in the 1850s, a practice that seems to have originated in continental Europe and then spread to the USA before being adopted in Britain. Such luxuries slowly extended to the second class and, in the 1870s, to third class also. On the Continent, heating the trains by steam pipes supplied from the locomotive was a quite common practice by the 1870s; the system was tried by the LNWR in 1872 but was

rejected in favour of foot-warmers. The same Railway's locomotive superintendent, Francis Webb, a prolific source of both practical and impractical ideas, developed the chemical footwarmer. This metal container held acetate of soda, a substance that could store heat, giving it out as it slowly liquefied. Passengers soon found that this heat lasted much longer than hot-water heat, and moreover could sometimes be revived by vigorous

shaking. However, in 1884 the Caledonian Railway introduced steam heating, which by the turn of the century was rapidly replacing the footwarmer.

The introduction of corridor trains simplified the operation of dining cars in long-distance trains. However, dining cars did exist before then; passengers would sit in them for the whole trip, or join them and leave them at intermediate stations (a practice still

Above: Three 'Harvey Girls' pose at the Santa Fe RR station at Rosenberg, Texas. Above right: A 'Harvey House' on the Santa Fe RR at Hutchinson, Kansas, in the mid 1920s.

followed in India). In the early years it was customary for trains to make scheduled meal stops at certain stations. Thus was born the railway refreshment room, at places such as Wolverton on the London & Birmingham, and Swindon on the Great Western. These refreshment rooms, run by private contractors, had to evolve new methods to handle large influxes of short-stay diners; one of their innovations was the bar, which enabled the greatest number of passengers to be served drinks and refreshments in the shortest possible time; this was soon copied by certain innkeepers and is now a permanent feature of the British scene. In time some refreshment rooms acquired a bad reputation for the quality of their food or service. Moreover, they were a hindrance when companies wished to accelerate their schedules, for there was little point in building powerful locomotives to haul faster trains when much of the journey time was spent at refreshment stops. However, easing out the contractors was not easy, and the GWR, for example, paid enormous compensation to the proprietors of the Swindon refreshment rooms when it decided to run trains non-stop through that station. On the longer hauls on American and Australian railways the meal stop was a welcome diversion for passengers, and it has not entirely disappeared. In America, especially, passengers soon learned to distrust the proprietors of lineside dining establishments, who all too frequently

took great advantage of their monopoly, cooking local rodents for their stews and serving their meals at high prices in fly-blown surroundings. It was an Englishman, Fred Harvey, who did most to rescue American station dining rooms. He contracted to operate such establishments on the new Santa Fe transcontinental railroad in the 1870s, and made a point of providing meticulous service with spotless white tablecloths and burnished silver cutlery. He also anticipated the airline hostess idea, employing the prettiest girls he could find as waitresses. These were the 'Harvey Girls', about whom countless ballads were written. So attractive and hardworking were these girls that Harvey had to include a clause in their contract which enabled him to claim back part of a girl's wages if she married and left before working a reasonable term for him. Soon other railroads had to follow the Harvey example, for the attraction of the Harvey Houses was drawing more and more passengers to the Santa Fe Railroad.

Because of its relatively short distances and high speeds, Britain did not feel a great need for sleeping car services and it was left to the USA and continental Europe to pioneer this form of travel. What was probably the world's first sleeping car was operated over the Harrisburg-Chambersburg line, later part of the Pennsylvania Railroad, in 1837. This was simply an ordinary day coach modified by division into four compartments, each with three bunks. Passengers did not undress but merely lay on the bunks, probably using their carpet bags as pillows. In 1857 the Great Western Railway of Canada introduced a much more sophisticated sleeping vehicle, but this was soon

surpassed by the work of George Pullman, who in 1858 converted two day coaches of the Chicago & Alton Railroad, so that facing seats could be converted into bunks, with additional hinged bunks let down to form upper berths. These were so successful that in 1863, Pullman built his *Pioneer*, the prototype of the standard Pullman sleeper, with longitudinal bunks, of which the upper was hinged and the lower convertible into seats. A central aisle, and heavy curtains to cover the berths, were the other features of this vehicle. Such vehicles, with the later addition of superior kinds of accommodation such as self-contained bedrooms, formed the sleeping car fleet which Pullman operated under contract on most US railroads. In Europe, the Belgian Georges Nagelmackers, learning from Pullman's experience, began in 1872 the enterprise which soon took the name of International Sleeping Car Company. This company built sleeping and dining cars which it operated under contract with various European railways, usually on international services. What was perhaps its most celebrated train, the 'Orient Express', began running between Paris and Constantinople in 1883. As with the Pullman services, the International Sleeping Car Company soon became associated with luxury, and the standard of its service and the design of its cars and their furnishing, were of a high standard.

In Britain the first true sleeping cars were introduced on the East Coast

Right: A British comment on the Midland Railway's new American sleeping cars.

THE GRAPHIC

AN ILLUSTRATED WEEKLY NEWSPAPER

VOL. X.—No. 260
Regd at General Post Office as a Newspaper

SATURDAY, NOVEMBER 21, 1874

PRICE SIXPENCE
Or by Post Sixpence Halfpenny

Sleeping Car—going to Bed.

Good night Ma

Dawn—Is it time to get up?

A Smoke

Private-Room

Very refreshing

Confound it! How the fellow snores

A quiet Luncheon

THE RAILWAY QUESTION—NOTES IN A PULLMAN PALACE CAR ON THE MIDLAND RAILWAY

Route in 1873, followed by similar cars on the West Coast a few months later. As with the continental railways, the compartment principle was adopted, with transverse berths. After the Anglo-Scottish trains, the 'Irish Mail' of the LNWR was the next train to be equipped with these vehicles. On the whole there was little scope for sleeping services in Britain, although the Great Western introduced sleeping vehicles on its lines from London to Cornwall and South Wales. From 1888 the British railways sporadically discussed the question of whether to provide sleepers for third class passengers, but it was not until 1928 that they finally did so. Their next decision was quicker, and taken in 1934, this was to provide hot water bottles on request, but only to first class passengers.

In Britain, and to some extent in continental Europe, successive innovations like train toilets, steam heating, and electric lighting typically found their first application on the royal trains; the latter might be regarded almost as testing vehicles and their royal occupants as guinea pigs. Queen Victoria, however, was not the most docile of guinea pigs. She was no great

Below: A highly-imagined picture intended to show Queen Victoria's first rail journey.

lover of innovation. There were times when she demanded that new-fangled devices be removed, and the old favourites restored; she did not take very kindly to electric light, and she peremptorily ordered the reintroduction of her accustomed oil lamps and candles when the London & North Western Railway's Carriage Department proudly installed electric reading lamps in the Royal carriage in the 1890s.

Royalty first began to ride the rails in 1842, when both the Dowager Queen Adelaide and the Queen herself had special carriages provided for them. For Queen Adelaide, the London & Birmingham Railway built a four-wheeler that was little more than an elaborate railborne version of a royal coach. But it did provide a bed and may be regarded as one of the predecessors of the modern sleeping car.

Prince Albert rode the rails some years before Queen Victoria. In fact he was still only the Queen's suitor when he made his first trip in November 1839 between Slough (the station for Windsor) and London. He made several longer trips after that, especially on the Great Western, and is quoted as saying after one trip 'Conductor, not quite so fast next time, please.' The Queen was finally persuaded by the Prince to make a trip in 1842. The GWR was notified on

Saturday 11 June that the Queen would travel from Slough to London the following Monday morning. This was short notice, but the Railway's management had long anticipated this situation and had a saloon car ready. So at the appointed time the locomotive *Phlegethan* was ready in Slough Station at the head of a seven-car royal train. Three of the vehicles were carriage trucks, on which the road carriages of the Queen's attendants were loaded. During this operation the Queen, instead of staying in the special royal apartment arranged in the station building, decided to walk about, examining the track and the train and asking questions. Finally with the Company's two great engineers, Brunel and Gooch, on the locomotive, the train moved off. Twenty-five minutes later it arrived punctually at Paddington Station where the platform was entirely covered with a red carpet. Not spending much time with the reception line of Company officials and their wives, or with the guard of honour, the Queen proceeded to Buckingham Palace. Soon after she wrote to King Leopold of Belgium '. . . We arrived here yesterday morning, having come by the railroad from Windsor, in half an hour, free from dust and crowd and heat, and I am quite charmed with it.'

She soon became a frequent railway traveller. For the railway companies concerned this was an excellent advertisement of the *propriety* of the new form of transport, and well worth the anxieties occasioned by the Queen's foibles.

This trip in 1842 was not the first time a monarch had travelled by rail in England; that distinction seems to have been won by the King of Prussia who, when in London to attend the christening of the Prince of Wales, several times travelled between Windsor and London in January of 1842. For the Queen's first trip a saloon coach was built, rather like the normal saloon coaches but fitted out with some luxury. As on subsequent royal journeys over this line, the locomotive superintendent, Daniel Gooch, drove the engine. Gooch, who one day would be the chairman of the Great Western, soon acquired great experience in handling royalty. The

most royal of his trains was that of May 1844 when, as he later recalled '. . . the late Emperor of Russia came over to stay with the Queen at Windsor. The King & Queen of Saxony were with her at the same time. I one day had charge of the engine when they came to London and back; in one carriage was the Queen of England & Prince Albert, King and Queen of Saxony, & the Emperor of Russia, with a large train of big wigs in attendance. This might fairly be called a royal train'.

In Victoria's time, each railway on which she was likely to travel maintained its own royal saloon, together with 'semi-royal' vehicles which would be included to form the royal train. Other railways usually kept a special saloon which, although available for private hire, could be quickly furnished to make a passable royal vehicle. The lines most frequently used by the Queen were the Great Western between Windsor and London, the West Coast and East Coast routes to Balmoral in Scotland, the London &

South Western for trips to her residence on the Isle of Wight, and the South Eastern for occasional excursions to the continent. On one of her earlier trips on the London & Birmingham Railway the Company provided a four-wheeler which was notable in that it was centrally heated, and presumably the very first steam heated vehicle to run on the railways. The equipment consisted of a small oil-burning boiler passing hot water through pipes laid between the two surfaces of the double floor, with brass gratings in the upper floor to allow the warm air to circulate. Inside the saloon there was a throne-like armchair upon which the Queen was intended to sit when in public, and a more comfortable sofa hidden discreetly behind curtains for use when travelling. The roof was domed, and on the roof the central ventilator outlet was disguised as a royal crown.

The London & South Western designed in the early 1840s a four-wheeler for taking the Queen to Gosport (for the Isle of Wight). This was

Above: The most religious of railway cars: Pope Pius IX's private saloon. The first Roman line was opened in 1856.

elaborately furnished with lace, tassels, and embroidery and, unlike other royal vehicles, was quite elaborately decorated with scrolls. Grand decoration of the exteriors of royal vehicles, both in Britain and on the Continent, was quite rare; although Pope Pius IX, who occasionally used to travel around the papal states distributing blessings from his own railway car, had a vehicle resembling a rather fanciful church in its decoration.

On the Great Western, the first royal saloon was also the first eight-wheeler; it had been built originally as an ordinary four-wheeler but as such its riding was not to Prince Albert's liking, so a new and very successful chassis was installed for Victoria's first trip. Soon the GWR built a bigger and better saloon. This, too, was an eight-wheeler and was interesting in that it possessed a quaint rooftop signal. This was operated from inside the saloon and consisted of a disc and crossbar whose positions could be witnessed by the train's travelling porter, who on the Great Western sat on the back of the engine tender to observe the train. In this way Victoria could indicate that she would like a little less speed. In general, the Queen liked rail travel; it was certainly better than her royal

yachts, which had been designed more to impress than to provide a smooth motion. On a train she was not seasick, but high speeds she detested. When the doughty North British Railway tried to make up lost time by some speedy running the Queen was not at all amused, and let the Company know it. In August 1852 the secretaries of the railways which had operated the royal train were shown a letter from Her Majesty's Equerry: 'I am desired to intimate Her Majesty's wish that the speed of the Royal Train on the 30th and 31st should on no account be increased at any one part of the line in order to make up for time lost by an unforeseen delay at another. . . . This order has probably arisen from one of the Directors telling Her Majesty last year that they had been driving the Train at the rate of *60 miles* an hour, a gratuitous piece of information which very naturally alarmed Her Majesty, although it was probably incorrect. . . .' The Queen believed that high speed caused accidents, and when a railway suffered a catastrophe she would instinctively attribute this to excessive speed. She was genuinely distressed when her subjects were killed in rail accidents, and was only half-wrong in her condemnation of high speed. After all, the higher the speed the more casualties there would be, irrespective of the cause of the accident, and these high

speeds were all too often the result not of passengers' wishes, but of the vanity or competitiveness of the railway companies and their officials.

It was the London & North Western Railway which built the finest royal vehicles. At one time, it had seemed that this Railway would not have much royal business, because the Queen found the East Coast Route much more attractive from the scenic point of view. But after the death of Prince Albert she could no longer endure the East Coast, because of its memories, and she transferred her patronage to the West Coast consortium. In 1861 the LNWR built a new four-wheeler, whose main compartment was intended for both day and night use. One practical drawback was that the Queen's compartment had no connection with other parts of the vehicle or with the rest of the train. This meant that in the morning and evening the Queen's dressing ladies had to get down on to the track and hoist themselves into the Queen's compartment in order to do their duties and footmen had the same problem. So after just a few years the LNWR devised something better. This was a pair of six-wheelers, the first in Britain to be joined by a gangway enclosed in bellows. The Queen never used this gangway when the train was in motion, but it was a great convenience for her attendants. One of the cars was fitted out as a day

VICTORIA'S DAY SALOON.

Above: Queen Victoria's day saloon in the LNWR Royal Train.

saloon, and the other was for night use, with a compartment for the dressing ladies attached. The Queen apparently liked this arrangement; it was built in 1869 and in 1895 was converted into a very fine single twelve-wheeler simply by joining the two bodies and placing them on a chassis consisting of two six-wheel bogies. The suppression of the bellows apparently gratified the Queen; she would no longer have to wait for an engine-changing stop in order to move between her day and night quarters. This vehicle is still in existence at the York National Railway Museum, and the richness of its interior furnishings can be seen in all their glory, except for some fading of colours. Much of this furnishing was not simply decorative; the thick carpet and the quilted silk coverings on the walls and ceiling were useful noise-inhibitors, and also helped to keep the vehicles warm. A somewhat similar vehicle was built for Queen Victoria's continental trips, being stored at Calais when not in use.

For other royalty visiting the continent another twelve-wheel saloon was built in 1883. It was similarly kept at Calais, the South Eastern Railway being made responsible for its upkeep. It was more practical than decorative in its interior arrangements, having sofas as berths,

and several portable tables. The Prince of Wales often used this saloon for his continental excursions, both before and after he succeeded his mother as King Edward VII. In April 1900 the future King Edward VII used this vehicle for a trip to Copenhagen. En route, he took a stroll on Brussels Station and after re-entering his royal saloon, found himself facing the barrel of a pistol poked through the open window by someone standing on the platform. One shot was fired before the stationmaster leapt on to the assailant, and that shot missed. The gunman was a 15-year-old 'anarchist', and Edward asked that he be not punished too severely in view of his age. In fact he went free, which prompted Kaiser Wilhelm to write sympathetically to Edward, denouncing the Belgian jury as a 'set of damned bloody scoundrels'.

In Britain, King Edward VII enjoyed yet another of the LNWR's royal trains, built in 1903. Apparently the new King did not appreciate his mother's taste in royal trains, and had asked for something less grandly furnished, more like one of his yachts. The nucleus of the new train was two royal saloons, each 65ft (19m) in length, one being for the King and the other for Queen Alexandra. Each had a day and a night room, with various offices and dressing rooms. To form the royal train, a first-class dining car, a couple of brake-first composites,

and six semi-royal cars were provided, the latter being for the royal suite. The entire eleven-car train was painted in the LNWR coaching livery of purple-brown and white. The semi-royal vehicles, when not required for their prime purpose, could be hired out as private vehicles to anybody rich enough to afford the minimum of twelve first-class tickets asked by the Company. This train lasted for four decades. It was only during World War II that the London Midland & Scottish Railway built a replacement for it.

Apart from the embarrassment of an assassination attempt at Brussels, there were few mishaps attending the operation of the royal trains. But they were a source of worry to railway managements, and all kinds of special arrangements were made, with the highest officials supervising them. It was quite common for the highest officers of the companies to travel with the trains, so as to be in a position to take instant decisions in the event of an emergency. One practice was the despatch of a 'pilot engine' a few minutes ahead of the royal train to check that the line was really clear. The worst that ever happened occurred on the West Coast Route, when in the early morning during a night trip to Scotland it was found that every one of the toilets on the Queen's train had frozen up.

Other monarchs were not quite so

lucky. Royal trains in Russia seemed to lead a rather dangerous life. In the very early days of the first main line, from St Petersburg to Moscow, the Tsar's train was delayed because the locomotive's wheels at one station slipped uncontrollably and could not be persuaded to grip the rails; it was discovered that a zealous stationmaster, an army man, had ordered the rails to be greased so they would shine more brightly. The same Tsar, Nicholas I. had two royal engines, 4-4-0s of American design; these had a rather heavy axle-load and, therefore a tendency to break the rails, so their wheel arrangement had to be changed to an ungainly 6-4-0. Nicholas I's successor Alexander II had even more hair-raising experiences. In the words of a South-Western Railway official: 'We were waiting on Zhmerinka station for the arrival of the Imperial Train. Suddenly, near the Zhmerinka station of the Kiev-Brest Railway, the Imperial Train ran off the rails. So the Emperor came to us at the station on foot. . . .' The Emperor's first question it seems was 'What happened?', and when he was persuaded that it had not been an act of 'evil intent' reacted quite generously, waiting patiently until the Imperial Train was replaced on the rails and he could continue his journey. On another occasion, on the same railway, the Tsar got out of his saloon for a stroll while engines were being changed. No doubt tired of bowing and scraping officials, he did this unobserved; the train was then signalled away, leaving the Tsar on the platform. The same Tsar used to make frequent train trips to the Crimea, and two trains were required for himself, his family and enormous suite, with all their baggage. On one occasion his second train, mainly carrying baggage and the Tsar's favourite foods and wines, was allowed to precede the imperial train. This was

an unusual stroke of good fortune, because for some weeks revolutionaries had been burrowing like moles under all the railway lines which the Tsar's train might take. They mistook the baggage train for the Tsar's train and set off their charge beneath it; the red stains spattered over the surrounding countryside were not the remains of the Tsar, but vestiges of his favourite Crimean plum jam.

Tsar Alexander III was the very opposite of Queen Victoria on the question of train speeds. If the Imperial Train did not attain the speed he considered fitting for the Emperor of All the Russias he felt affronted and vented his displeasure on the railway officials and directors who accompanied his train. His desire for speed was a kind of vanity. On one occasion he ordered a special train with relays of fast engines to bring him a spare uniform from St Petersburg to the Ukraine, where he was attending army manoeuvres, in forty-eight hours. In 1888, en route to Kiev, his train was so heavy that the fearful railway officials provided two freight engines for it to ensure the required speed. Travelling at high speed, the small wheels of these locomotives, with their heavy balancing weights, must have inflicted enormous 'hammerblow' stresses on the rails, and eventually, passing over a length where the wooden sleepers were half rotten, a rail broke. In the resulting derailment 21 persons were killed. The royal family was in the dining car and the heavily-built Tsar supported the roof of this collapsing vehicle with his shoulders while the family escaped.

These were not the only mishaps to Russian royal trains. On one ceremonial visit, after the train had slowly drawn up so that the door of the Royal saloon faced a special red-carpeted platform, the door refused to open, and royalty had to scramble down elsewhere. The

Russian royal train that was kept in Germany for the European travels of the imperial family suffered an explosion while awaiting the arrival of an empress at Rostock; new-fangled American electric generators were blamed for this. All in all, it seemed quite appropriate that the last Tsar would sign his abdication while marooned in the royal train after vainly attempting to reach the capital.

The running of royal trains was far removed from the railways main function as provider of mass transport. So far as passengers were concerned, the handling of masses of people by the trainload meant not only the provision of suitable trains, but also the development of new ways of dealing with large numbers of people. Thus in such matters as the issue of tickets, the design of stations, and the advertisement of train services, fresh thinking was needed.

Early ticketing arrangements at first followed the practice of the road coaches. Tickets were written out by hand and numbered to correspond with a vacant seat in a particular train. But as travellers increased, a better method was needed. Speed of ticket issue was important; no passenger wished to spend half an hour or more waiting for his turn at the ticket table, and no railway wanted to maintain an enormous army of ticket clerks simply to reduce this waiting time. Moreover, binding a ticket to a particular seat number made difficult the issue of return tickets and it deprived the passenger of what would become and remain the great advantage of rail travel in most countries, the ability to travel on any train according to the passenger's own convenience. Being mass carriers, railways were able to stand the cost of providing far more seats than were really required, and this margin was of enormous importance because it enabled railways to dispense with the need to insist on passengers reserving their places. It was not long before railway companies realized this, and they abandoned compulsory reservations.

A big step forward was the invention of the familiar pre-printed cardboard ticket by Charles Edmondson of the Newcastle & Carlisle Railway. With a simple manually-operated date-stamping machine a ticket clerk simply selected the required ticket from his ticket rack, date-stamped it, and sold it to the client. All tickets were numbered in series, and were drawn from their

racks in numerical order, so that recording the issue of each ticket was no longer necessary; it was sufficient at the end of the day to record the serial numbers of the last tickets sold of each category. Station booking offices had stocks of printed tickets to cover almost all destinations that would be required. For passengers booking to an unexpected destination there was a supply of tickets in which the destination and fare could be written in by hand, and this was the only concession that the Edmondson system made to the old methods. Edmondson was soon lured away from the Newcastle & Carlisle Railway by a higher salary offered by the Lancashire & Yorkshire, which exploited his system to the full. It was soon copied by other railways, and the card tickets are still known as 'Edmondson tickets'. Edmondson, unlike many inventors employed by British firms, did secure royalties, and lived comfortably for the rest of his life.

The Edmondson ticket is still widely used; even many types of automatic ticket-issue systems still use it. In America it was supplemented by the coupon paper ticket, in which tear-off portions of a ticket were provided for each section of a journey. This was particularly useful when a through journey was made over the tracks of more than one company. Train conductors could then remove the section of the ticket applying to the run over their own particular lines, and in due course this part of the ticket would be presented for payment to the company that issued the ticket. As in Edmondson's system, a great advantage of this method was the reduction in clerical tasks that it permitted.

The Edmondson and the coupon ticket may be regarded as the basic types, but there were many variations. Within each system, modifications were introduced to suit particular requirements. With the card tickets, the use of distinctive colours for particular types of ticket soon became widespread; this again lightened the load of railway employees, especially ticket inspectors who could tell at a glance, without

reading the inscription, whether a ticket was of first or third class, whether it was a cheap return, and so on. With commuter, or season, tickets, some companies dispensed with the Edmondson system, issuing card tickets that were somewhat larger than standard. In some parts of the world metal discs took the place of card tickets when three-month or one-year periods of travel were purchased by regular travellers. Such tickets were similar to the discs issued by companies as free passes to certain of their officials or, sometimes, to useful individuals like bankers and industrialists. Typically a disc pass enabling the holder to travel anywhere, in any train, on any date, was of silver.

In their efforts to tap new sources of traffic, the railways over the decades introduced all kinds of concessionary fares. In Britain, up to 1928, each company had a maximum fare scale fixed by its act of parliament. Few companies charged the maximum, and there was no restriction on how little they might charge. There was no standardization among companies, nor

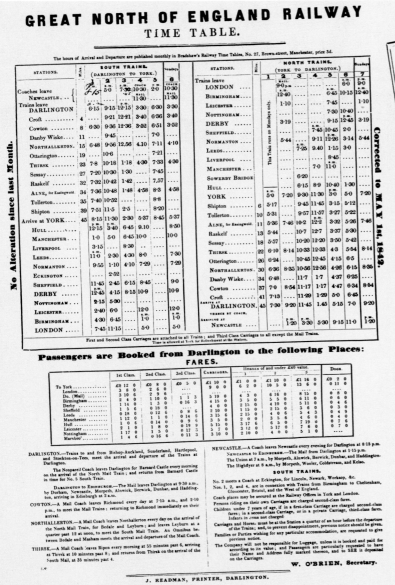

GREAT NORTH OF ENGLAND RAILWAY
TIME TABLE.

BRADSHAW'S RAILWAY GUIDE;

CONTAINING

A CORRECT ACCOUNT OF THE HOURS OF ARRIVAL AND DEPARTURE OF THE TRAINS ON EVERY RAILWAY IN GREAT BRITAIN;

A MAP OF ENGLAND,

WITH THE RAILWAYS COMPLETED AND IN PROGRESS,

HACKNEY COACH FARES, &c.

FOR DECEMBER, 1841.

MANCHESTER:

PRINTED & PUBLISHED BY BRADSHAW & BLACKLOCK, 27, BROWN-ST.
AND SOLD BY
W. J. ADAMS, 170, FLEET STREET, LONDON,
AND MAY BE HAD THROUGH ALL BOOKSELLERS AND NEWSMEN.

Above: One of the early issues of *Bradshaw's Railway Guide*, a national railway timetable including all companies and independently published.
Left: A typical railway company timetable: this early British example is of the short-lived Great North of England Railway, soon to become the North Eastern Railway.

did each company apply a fixed rate per mile; the circumstances of the market, and especially the competitive situation, were very influential. In 1865, of the large companies, the Caledonian was the cheapest *on average*, charging 0.7 pence per mile for third class, 1.1 pence for second, and 1.2 pence for first. Unlike several of the larger companies, the Caledonian did not have a higher scale of charges for travel by fast train. Among the most expensive railways was the Great Eastern, which charged 2.8 pence for first class travel by fast train, did not offer third class accommodation in such trains, and charged the maximum allowable (one penny per mile) for third class travel on ordinary trains. Some companies offered a reduction for return tickets, but others did not. After the Midland Railway in 1872 initiated the practice of taking third class passengers in all trains, and then in 1875 of renaming second class as third class, the railways began to apply new rates per mile, but again these were not standardized between companies. Only after World War I was a country-wide standard rate

established of 1½ pence per mile in third class and 2½ pence in first, but the four big railway companies later agreed to introduce cheaper rates for what they called 'monthly returns'.

Special excursion tickets must date from the very beginning of the railway age, when very cheap, or even free, travel might be offered at the inauguration of a new railway. Apart from these events, the first true excursion train may have been that operated by the Bodmin & Wadebridge Railway in 1836, when a single fare was charged for the double journey. The same Railway later ran an excursion to take passengers to see a public execution, and as the Railway passed alongside Bodmin prison the lucky passengers were able to view the spectacle while remaining in their seats. In 1841 Thomas Cook ran his first chartered-train as a kind of excursion, and since that time, except in wartime, excursions have proved a useful way of increasing passenger revenue by utilizing rolling stock and track capacity at off-peak periods.

Excursions, typically, were advertised

in local newspapers, and this medium was the most common in the early years for advertizing regular passenger schedules. However, as services grew more complex, and as travellers moved greater distances from the areas covered by their local press, something better was needed. The railway timetable boom was the answer. Each company, apart from pasting poster-size timetables on its stations, printed such timetables in reduced format to form books or pamphlets, which could then be distributed, free or otherwise, to potential passengers. The famous national railway timetable, *Bradshaw's Guide*, appeared quite early in the history of British Railways. George Bradshaw was an engraver of Manchester, specializing in maps of canals and railways, and in 1838 he decided to take into partnership the printer William Blacklock. The pair began to publish canal and railway directories and guides, including a quarterly railway guide and timetable. This latter proved very popular and in 1844 the partners were able to make it a monthly publication. This established itself as Britain's national railway timetable, and survived until 1961, even though it had to compete with the individual railway companies' own timetables. Although the presentation of trains in the timetables in the form of vertical columns of arrival and departure times was not originated by *Bradshaw's Guide*, the partners were responsible for the complex system of footnotes and symbols which enabled the maximum information to be presented in the smallest possible space. However, this proliferation of symbols, plus the vertical presentation, baffled many users, and was a regular target for satirical comment in *Punch*. Later, there appeared *Bradshaw's Continental Guide*, and *Bradshaw's Guides* appeared in other countries, including Australia. Of these, *Newman's Indian Bradshaw* still survives. Another well-known timetable was *Cook's Continental Timetable*, which still flourishes, and which now occupies the place once held by *Bradshaw's Continental Guide*. In the USA, as in Britain, the individual railways published their own timetables despite the availability of commercial editions.

Standardization of technique and equipment was an early feature of the railways, but stations were an exception, for there was no great economy to be gained by standardizing their design. Although from time to time architects, railway administrators, and Russian Tsars dreamed up standard designs for stations to be duplicated all over a given system, most railway stations had their own individuality. Even when standardization was aimed at, local circumstances usually ensured that there would be local variations too.

As in other respects, the first railway companies proceeded by trial and error in their provision of stations, with the trend ever towards more ambitious architecture and services. Many railways in the early days thought it sufficient to imitate the stage coaches, stopping their train near a particular inn, where booking would be done. But by the time the Liverpool & Manchester Railway was undertaken there were railway promoters and engineers with other ideas. A boarding platform, an awning to keep off the rain, a place to wait, a place to buy tickets and, at terminals, a place to store rolling stock seemed to be the essentials. Less essential, but convenient, was the incorporation of railway offices in the station, this provided the opportunity to construct a large building of some degree of impressiveness. At first separate departure and arrival

Above right: Paddington Station: the iron and glass roof is broken by this transept, which formerly spanned the turntables.
Right: Frith's famous painting of Paddington Station in 1862.

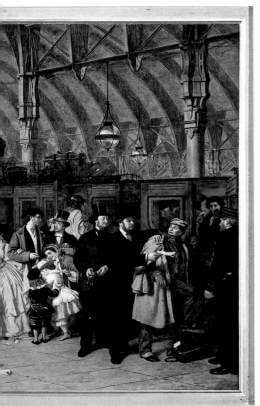

platforms were not provided and moreover, when they were, some engineers preferred a single long platform with a scissors crossing in the middle, enabling two trains travelling in opposite directions to use the platform at the same time (an arrangement that survives, notably at Cambridge, England). But different platforms for different directions soon became the most usual arrangement. How those platforms were covered provided scope for individual preferences and, as the decades passed, for even more astonishing feats of engineering. At first a barn-like structure straddling both the platform and the tracks was quite common. As in other matters of architecture, farm buildings were the inspiration of railway architects, and the term 'train barn' can still be encountered in America. Later, after the Great Exhibition had shown what could be done with iron and glass, the all-over arched roof became popular. An early example of this was built at Paddington Station by the Great Western Railway. At about the same time Lewis Cubitt built the King's Cross Terminus for the Great Northern Railway. This had two 105ft (32m) spans resting on arcaded walls, with their outline carried through to the front of the station building. It is said that Cubitt was inspired by the Tsar's riding stables in Moscow, and that King's Cross was an imitation of the latter, but although there is an external resemblance, presumably intended, the engineering fundamentals are very different. Cubitt was of a well-known family of civil engineers; it had been William Cubitt who had testified in Parliament to show that George Stephenson's survey for the Liverpool & Manchester Railway was incompetent. Apart from King's Cross, Lewis Cubitt was the originator of what became known as the 'English Railway Style', station buildings based on old Italian architecture.

There were three main variables in designing a city station: layout; the design of the buildings, and notably the facade; and the form of the roofing over the platforms, that is, the design of the train-shed. These three choices could be described as, respectively, operating, architectural, and engineering. That different kinds of talents were called for is emphasized by the tendency for the station buildings to be designed by an architect, and the train-shed by an engineer. A notable example of this is St Pancras in London. Here the enormously wide arched iron roof, a single span of 243ft (74m) without any crossties (the station platforms acting as braces, with the foundation of the arches well below platform level) was designed by William Barlow. Whereas a majority of the engineers and architects who built the larger stations were not specialists in railway work, Barlow was a resident engineer of the Midland Railway and later, for almost fifty years, was consultant to that Company. It was only after the great Barlow roof had been designed that the Railway entrusted the celebrated architect Gilbert Scott with the offices and hotel that were to form the head and facade of this great station. Scott had recently submitted two designs for the new Foreign Office building, and his preferred version, a palatial neo-Gothic redbrick structure which would have dominated Whitehall and been a grand memorial to himself, had been rejected in favour of the more modest version. The St Pancras commission gave him a chance to soothe his disappointment and to show what a great chance the government had missed by rejecting his grand design; when finished, the redbrick neo-Gothic pile of St Pancras Station could be recognized as a railway version of Scott's proposed Foreign Office.

The wooden train-shed was quite common for big city stations in the early decades of the railway age, and sometimes for medium sized stations later. Many such stations survived on the Great Western Railway until they were closed in the economy drive of the 1960s. In America they were rather more common and, because American locomotives burned wood and emitted more sparks, often caught fire. Possibly the best place to see such stations is now Australia, where Ballarat has a good example. However, both America and Australia soon entered the age of the iron arched roof. Brisbane had an interesting semi-elliptical span of about 100 feet (30.48m), while different American companies began to compete in the extent they could enclose beneath their iron and glass structures. The second Philadelphia (Broad Street) station of 1893 had a single span roof of no less than 300 feet (91.44m). In Germany, too, the iron roof was highly developed. Hamburg, built in 1906, had a single span roof 240 feet (73.15m) wide. The German arched roof was notable for its solidity, much more iron being used than was really necessary; and in World War II, the glassless, damaged, but still-standing station roof was often the most prominent structure to survive in badly bombed German cities.

Station layouts grew larger and more complex as the decades passed, but

little that was revolutionary could be attempted here, for operating needs changed little. The early practice of using spare tracks for the storage of rolling stock proved to be most useful because, when increased traffic demanded more platforms, carriage storage could be moved out down the line and the space freed for new platforms. It was because of this that a number of British city stations never required extensive extension. At terminals there was always the question of whether to place the main building at the side of the tracks, or at the head end, beyond the buffers; the latter was usually chosen, except when there was a possibility of a line extension later. Eventually the most fitting layout, aesthetically and practically, was found to be a U-shaped block, both heading and flanking the tracks. A notable development was the introduction of a passenger circulating area, or concourse, between the tracks and the station building. At terminals the ideal place for this was, obviously, behind the buffers. It appears to have been the French who introduced the concourse in 1847 for the Nord Railway's Paris

terminal, although two of the biggest concourses can be seen at Leipzig in Germany and Waterloo Station in London. The Grand Central Terminal of New York Central is a slightly different case, for its circulating area, apart from being enormous, is divided and subdivided. Leipzig is also a good example of a layout which became quite common in Germany, where each train would enter on a single track between two platforms, with one platform being used by the passengers and the other by the mail and parcels staff. This segregation of passengers from mail and parcels was not adopted in Britain, which is why, at times, British passenger terminals resembled goods stations, with passengers making their way perilously between heaps of mailbags and moving columns of parcels' trolleys.

To meet local needs there were, of course, unusual layouts. The bi-level station was one; this was used where two lines crossed each other more or less at right angles, so that some platforms had to be built not only at a higher level but at an angle to the lower level platforms. Tamworth was a good example of this arrangement, where the Midland Railway crossed the main line of the London & North Western Railway near Birmingham. This particular station

was a favourite haunt of train watchers right up to the end of steam (or rather, until British Railways prohibited train-watching there). At junctions, platforms would sometimes be built alongside the divergent lines, forming an apex in which, typically, the station building would be erected. There were a few cases of triangular stations, built alongside the tracks of three lines. Notably, perhaps the most unusual layout was to be found at Asunción, in Paraguay. Here the terminus had one line continuing past the buffer stops, through the end of the station, across a main road, through a wall, and into the army barracks. The railway was built by the dictator Carlos Lopez and he wanted to be absolutely sure there was no delay in sending off troops by rail to quell any disturbance threatening his rules. Running one or two lines through the buildings at the end of a terminal was not unknown elsewhere. In America a line might emerge in this way and then run down the main street, sharing the latter with pedestrians and motor vehicles. An early Leipzig station in Germany had a turntable in front of the station building and a popular pastime for passers by at that time was to watch an engine emerging from the station through an arcade and an iron

gateway, and then being turned.

It was the station building which offered architects and their clients the best opportunity for creating an impression. The railway offices which the Liverpool & Manchester Railway provided alongside its Liverpool station were modest, providing accommodation only. But it was not long before railway managements decided that a station building could be designed to influence people. Notable among the early terminals built to impress as well as to serve was Euston of the London & North Western Railway. This had not only its Great Hall to accommodate waiting passengers under a magnificently ornate ceiling, but also possessed what was later known as the Euston Arch. This enormous and solid-looking arch was built at the entrance to the station and was virtually an *arc de triomphe*; some commentators believe it was to symbolize the conquest of London by the new age of the railway, but more likely it was to persuade the Railway's users that they were engaged in the conquest of time and space. However this attitude did not last, and mid-century marked the end of the heroic

age for the railways, and for their architecture. In later years the railways were less conquering and more commercial, with a corresponding loss of self-confidence. Nothing could be more symbolic of this loss of confidence than the decision in 1870, decades after its construction, to inscribe on the world-famous Euston Arch, in enormous letters, the word 'Euston'.

Of all the big British stations it is perhaps unfair to single out just two examples of the magnificent, designed-to-impress, facade. But Huddersfield, with its 416 foot long Corinthian frontage and central portico supported by eight columns, built in 1847, is surely deserving. So, too, is Newcastle Central, the masterpiece of perhaps the greatest British railway architect, John Dobson of Newcastle. Dobson, like so many of his contemporaries, was a man of many parts. Not only did he design station buildings; he replanned Newcastle's city centre, and his design of semi-elliptical arched iron roof was used for many stations in the North-East. However, the frontage and roofs of Newcastle Central make Dobson's masterpiece, even though the railway management's hesitations prevented him carrying out his original intentions to the full; and even though the portico was designed

and built during Dobson's last illness by a somewhat inferior architect.

By the end of the 19th century there was an attempt to return to the heroic style, but the result was all too often mere ostentation, through size or decoration, with the interests of the passenger taking second place. The final edition of Grand Central Terminal in New York, magnificent though it was, was only a manifestation of the New York Central Railroad president's wish to possess the world's most outstanding station; and Grand Central is not particularly convenient for a passenger in a hurry. Only the Milan (Central) Terminal, designed by Ulisse Stacchini and completed in 1930, can rival Grand Central in the imposing obstacles placed between a late-arriving passenger and his train. This was and remains, one of the problems of grandiose stations; in the attempt to impress it was forgotten that the basic function of a station is to provide a convenient meeting place for passenger and train.

Another way to impress was to borrow architectural or decorative motifs from another country. Sometimes this was done tastefully, as with the saracenic elements to be seen in the iron columns supporting the roof of

Above: The famous Euston Arch, leading to the LNWR's London terminus.

Paddington station. And sometimes, even when tasteless, an exciting result could be achieved, as at the Union Station in New Haven, Connecticut, where Italian, Moorish and oriental features were combined in a breathtaking mixture. Italianate features, including towers, were a feature of many British railway stations, especially those of medium and smaller towns. When British engineers and architects were set the task of designing stations for the Empire their imagination was unbounded and they produced quite fantastic designs that would never have been acceptable at home. The terminus of the Great Indian Peninsula Railway at Bombay has been described as an oriental St Pancras, while the station at Kuala Lumpur in Malaya seemed to be derived from some fairy-tale impression of an eastern palace.

By 1914 railway station architecture had become static. There was a limit to ostentation and that limit had been reached; only tasteless excess lay farther along that road. It was precisely at this point that a completely new approach was tried, beginning with

Saarinen's new terminus at Helsinki. This station retained the old status symbol of a tower, but in all else it was different. It was functional instead of ornate; it made good use of local materials; and it was well proportioned. There was an enormous concourse area, covered by a lofty arched roof and extending the full width of the station. Under the cover of this roof the passenger could do all he needed or wished to do, except actually board the train. The platforms only function was access to trains, and to help ensure that people would not linger on them they were provided with absolutely no cover from the elements. This station, being completed just as Finland obtained her independence from Russia, also became something of a national monument. In subsequent years and decades, functionalism of this kind became the main trend in new station design, at least in Europe. Later, when concrete and glass became fashionable, these new materials were combined with the functional philosophy to produce striking postwar stations such as the one in Rome, and the new Euston Station in London.

A common type of city station in both the USA and Britain was that which was

designed and used by several companies. Such stations were termed 'joint' in Britain and 'Union' in the USA. In the earlier decades competing and even cooperating companies felt it somehow undignified to share their premises, and there was many a city with three or four stations. This was neither convenient for passengers, who had to make their way from one station to another in order to continue their journey, nor inexpensive for the companies, since the cost of maintaining a station was very high. In the second half of the 19th century these basic facts began to make an impression on the companies, and joint stations were sometimes built. Such stations, whose design usually had to be approved by a committee, were unlikely to be revolutionary from the architectural point of view, but their interior workings were often very lively. In Britain, Carlisle was the most rewarding of the joint stations for a train watcher, for it was used by the passenger services of no fewer than seven English and Scottish companies, each in their own distinctive colours and using their individual designs of locomotive and rolling stock. In the USA the enormous terminus of St Louis Union Station had a

THE GREAT CENTRAL RAILWAY STATION AT NEWCASTLE-UPON-TYNE.

Above: The facade of Newcastle Central Station, designed by John Dobson.

similarly wide display of rolling stock.

Britain was very distinctive in its treatment of the small stations. Quite apart from the fact that only in Britain did every station have its platforms raised almost to the level of the train's floor, the variety of architectural styles was unmatched elsewhere. There were so many different companies and so many different architects, while each station seemed to have its own local peculiarity demanding special treatment. Perhaps the most common feature, and one in which it was possible to experiment with all kinds of variations, was the veranda-type awning over the platforms. These awnings were often cantilevered out from the station building, but sometimes they were supported by columns along the platform. The design of the awnings and of their columns was unique to each railway. Around the awning, almost always, was a vertical skirt, or valance, and this was cut to form a repetitive and decorative pattern which, too, varied from company to company and sometimes from station to station. The broad awning, stretching up to the

track, and its valance, meant that a passenger could board a train without encountering a single raindrop, except when it was windy.

British small-town stations, unlike those of the cities, usually avoided ostentation. The ideal seemed to be a station that would blend perfectly into its surroundings. Because the railways were regarded by many as an unsightly intrusion which destroyed the countryside there was no doubt a good reason for harmonizing the stations, and this was done by building them in the style of a country house (for the larger stations) and of a country cottage (for the small). While each company eventually developed its own 'house-style' in matters such as the design of awnings, seats, lettering, lamps, and nameboards, so that a passenger could feel at a glance on whose company's property he had alighted, there was still a difference between stations on the same line. This was true even when a standard 'unit' building had been adopted for all stations, as on the London, Brighton & South Coast Railway.

In continental Europe, there seemed to be much more uniformity. Some attributed this to the more bureaucratic approach, with stations being

designated as of First, Second or Third rate significance with an appropriate range of standard facilities laid down for each category. But even there, apart from national differences, there were differences of age, for many of the earliest stations, erected before the bureaucratic mind took over, survived. In America wooden construction was almost universal, and each station consisted of certain basics like the despatchers' office, the woodburning Dutch stove, and the low or non-existing platform.

In Britain (and in her empire too), there were important terminological differences which foreigners sometimes found baffling. If a station's name ended in 'Road', as in Pontypool Road or Gwinear Road, it meant that it was several, or many, miles from the town mentioned in the first part of its name. There was also the distinction accorded by the title of 'halt' rather than 'station'. The halt was intended for light traffic, was usually unstaffed, and did not provide such facilities as toilets. Usually all it consisted of was a platform and a hut which afforded some protection from the elements for the waiting passengers; it was a particularly useful form of structure when a new area was being developed and the railway was not sure whether enough traffic would be forthcoming to justify a station. Some companies, notably the Great Western, had an even lower designation, 'platform', which often provided nothing but that, and at which intending passengers were bidden to signal an approaching train if they wanted it to stop for them.

Passenger trains and stations were concerned not only with passengers, nor was their revenue derived solely from the carriage of people. Being the fastest trains on a railway, the passenger services also conveyed commodities for which rapid delivery was important. Parcels were, and still are, a good example. Newspapers, too, were a significant source of revenue.

But the most important non-passenger traffic was mail. In some countries, Germany and Russia in particular, governments favoured railway construction largely because this would mean an acceleration of mail services, and early railways were required to carry government mails free of charge or at very reduced rates. Most railways sent their mail traffic by the fastest train; indeed, the fastest trains were often introduced simply to satisfy the post office, which demanded tight schedules in exchange for the valued mail contract. In time, and especially in North America, it was the mail contract which enabled some passenger trains to continue running, because the passengers, alone, were too few to cover operating costs.

In the early years mail was carried on the railways in ordinary road mail coaches, mounted on 'carriage trucks' (flatcars) for the rail part of their journey. Mail coaches in Britain were painted red, and this colour was used for the later, specially built, railway mail vehicles. In cases where only a part of a railway vehicle was used for mail, that part only would be painted red, a practice which still survives in India and elsewhere.

In 1838 the Travelling Post Office concept made its debut on the Grand Junction Railway in Britain. Between Birmingham and Liverpool a converted horse box was used not simply for the carriage of mail, but also for its sorting en route. Rows of pigeon holes along the interior walls of this vehicle enabled

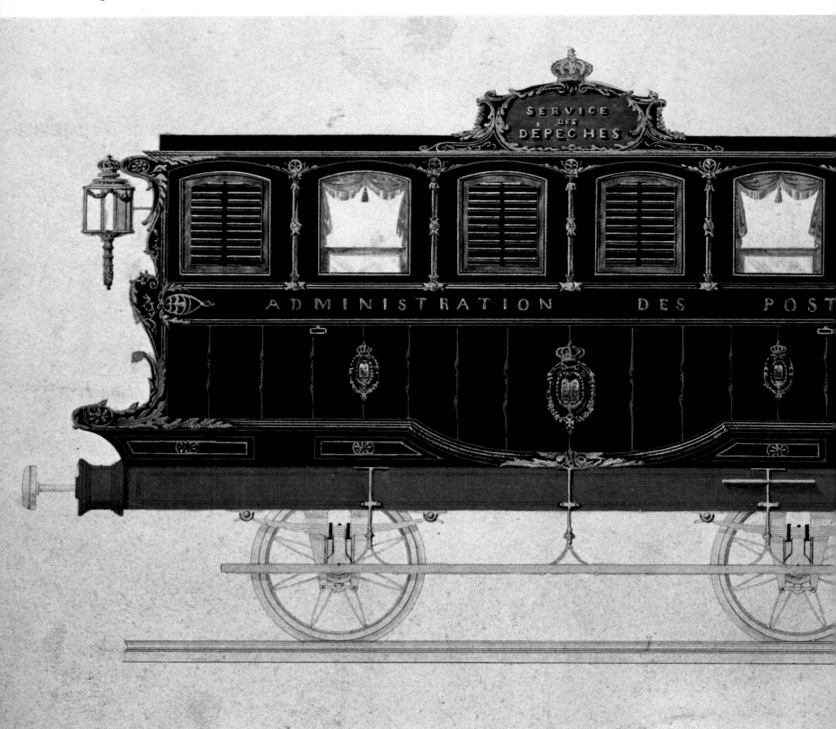

the post office clerks to sort the letters, aided by a level of illumination rather superior to that offered to passengers. To save even more time, apparatus was devised for picking up and setting down mail without the train stopping. A folding net swung out from the side of the car caught up a pouch of mail suspended at the lineside from automatic release clips. From the train a pouch was slid down a chute into a net waiting at the lineside. However, as

Right: Passenger trains also carried parcels. This overhead parcels carrier at Manchester Victoria (L & Y Rly) left the station platforms clear for passengers.
Below: An early continental European postal car. Such cars were often owned by the government postal administrations, which also staffed them.

train speeds increased accurate timing became difficult; postmen waiting at the lineside sometimes were sent flying by a pouch released a fraction of a second too late. For this reason the chute delivery was abandoned, and the lineside apparatus snatched rather than passively accepted the train's pouch. In 1855 the first all-mail train was introduced on the Great Western between London and Bristol; such trains still run on British Rail although they are no longer painted red, and pouch exchange at speed is no longer practised. Elsewhere in Europe the Travelling Post Office idea spread rapidly. Special vehicles were used, brightly painted as in Britain (although orange seems to have been the favoured colour). Mail vehicles featured a letter slot, into which the public could slip their letters and thereby catch the last post. In the USA the first travelling post office was scheduled by the Hannibal & St Joseph Railroad in 1861.

Although railways tended to be judged by their passenger services, most companies derived the greater part of their revenue from freight. There were some railways, like the London, Brighton & South Coast in Britain and the Long Island Railroad in the USA, which were mainly passenger railways, but these were exceptions. Among railways which did carry passengers, but were overwhelmingly concerned with freight, were the North Eastern Railway in England, several coal-hauling lines in South Wales, and companies like the Norfolk & Western hauling Appalachian coal down to America's Atlantic seaboard. By the turn of the century the USA was technically far in advance of Britain and Europe in freight haulage. It had long standardized the high-capacity boxcar, running on two four-wheel trucks, whereas in Europe the long wheelbase four-wheeler and in Britain the short four-wheeler were still used. In Britain the low-capacity freight car was destined to survive until the present day. Some railway companies, realizing how uneconomical such cars could be, tried to introduce larger vehicles which could carry more tons of freight per ton of vehicle. But the prevalence in Britain of the so-called private owner wagon meant that such efforts produced few results. Private-owner wagons were exactly what their name indicated, freightcars owned not by a railway but by a shipper. In Britain the private coalmining companies were among the largest wagon-owners; the different liveries of their wagons certainly enlivened freightyards, but these vehicles were very uneconomical and it was virtually impossible to

persuade the mineowners to introduce bigger or better cars. Cars carrying ten tons of coal were very suited to the operations of collieries, with their light curved tracks and primitive loading installations, but they were hardly suited to mass transport operations.

British freightcars were archaic by other standards too. Whereas in the USA the automatic coupler and the Westinghouse air brake by which the locomotive crew could apply brakes down the whole length of their trains were standard equipment by the end of the 19th century, in Britain a three-link chain dropped over a hook was the usual coupling, and brakes were operated by hand on each car. Stopping a British freight train was accomplished by the locomotive brakes and the brakes of the four-wheel van at the rear where the train guard was required to attend to the brakes as well as watch the train. When a steep gradient had to be descended the train was stopped at the summit, and a brakeman proceeded down the train, pinning down a certain proportion of the handbrakes. This far from ideal way of operating freight trains persisted for a long time in Britain, and in fact can still be witnessed with certain municipal trains. The charge that British railways were too intent on spending money and ingenuity in glamorous enterprises, like streamlined trains, and too little interested in improving really basic defects, is difficult to refute.

Yet while British railway companies seemed indifferent to the persistence of dangerous and uneconomic practices like hand-braked trains and loose chain couplings, the same companies and their engineers led the world in the development of safer railway signalling. Collisions were the most feared kind of railway accident and the technique of train separation underwent improvements as successive methods were found to be not quite adequate. Maintaining a time interval between trains was one early technique which sometimes failed when a train was stopped between stations for some unexpected reason and at once became vulnerable to a rear-end collision. So the time interval system was replaced by the space interval, and various means of signalling were evolved to ensure that the intervals were maintained. The key innovation was the block system, in which a line was divided into sections, or 'blocks', and no train was allowed to enter one block until the preceding train had left it. This entailed the setting up of control points (signal boxes in Britain) at the boundaries of the blocks. These control

points were in telegraphic communication with their neighbours and operated signals to communicate with train crews. In time the semaphore signal, worked by a lever and wire, became the favourite, although in France the revolving disc and board was the chosen type. In America train control was somewhat different, because distances were great and most routes were single track. With Samuel Morse's telegraph connecting the stations, 'despatchers' at those stations could plan train movements. A train crew would receive written 'train orders', picked up without stopping at passing stations, if the normal schedule had to be altered. However, America in 1865 did adopt the block system for certain busy double track lines, being encouraged to do so by a very bloody accident when two troop trains collided in New Jersey.

The telegraph, first introduced by the Great Western Railway in 1839, was not foolproof; human error could still allow a train into an already occupied block section. Nor was the telegraph the final answer to operations on single-track lines. For the latter, a British engineer devised the token system. A token was the engine crew's authority to move into a section, and a machine was devised in which the tokens were normally kept. Neither this machine, in electrical communication with similar machines installed at the farther ends of the neighbouring sections, nor those other machines, could issue a token until the preceding token had been replaced in one or other of them.

A frequent human-error kind of accident was the setting of signals and points and switches in conflict, so that, for example, two trains might be given clearance to proceed over a junction at the same time. Another British invention, the Saxby interlocking frame, dealt with this. This frame was a mechanical contrivance which, when a given signal was put in the 'proceed' position, locked all switches and signals which, if changed, would conflict with that initial signal indication.

Successive improvements like the use of power-operated signals and the replacement of semaphore signals by coloured-lights, were important but not fundamental improvements of the interlocked block signalling system. What was last to be devised was a means of preventing accidents caused by locomotive crews failing to obey signals. This lack was remedied in the early 20th century with various forms of 'cab-signalling' and 'automatic train control'. These systems usually relied on electromagnetic signals transmitted

Above: Inside the signal box at Crewe North (LNWR). Such levers, operating semaphore signals, are still widely used, although the Crewe installation has been replaced.

to passing locomotives by trackside installations, the messages being determined by the aspect of the neighbouring semaphore or coloured-light signal. In this way it was possible for a locomotive crew to be informed of the aspect of a signal which might be invisible because of fog, and the more sophisticated systems could automatically apply the brake should a train pass a signal at danger. The Great Western Railway was a pioneer in this form of signalling, and was rewarded in the first half of this century with an accident rate noticeably lower than that of the other British companies.

Different countries, and different companies, were very individualistic in their signalling. The style of semaphore signals was, for example, a distinguishing characteristic of each British railway company. Some countries, moreover, continued to use

white as the 'all-clear' colour instead of green. Most countries did standardize the basic signal indications, so as to avoid possible confusion, but not all. Even today some US railroads have signal indications different from those of their neighbours. But this is not important so long as train crews are changed at railroad frontier points. This was not always recognized, and at a station used by several companies confusion was sometimes possible. This is alluded to in the following words of a Saxony railway minister, writing in 1870, whose anxieties are a reminder that the variety and individualism of the different railways, which seem so attractive nowadays, were not always welcome, especially to military planners wondering how the railways would function during wartime, under military control:

'. . . the military official is unfavourably placed. Every regulation which he discovers about the railway system – its station arrangements, its officials'

uniforms, its signals – is only of use for an hour or so while his troops are passing over it. Then there comes another railway with its own and often very different regulations. . . . At the big junction stations used by several companies, where at night the engineman sees a hundred different signals in bewildering confusion, which resemble stars that, because of the motion of the engine over the station's curves, seem to float backwards and forwards, merging into each other, one can often find lines running close to each other on one of which a white light signifies 'stop!' and on the other means 'line clear' . . . it would be to the general good in peacetime, and of benefit to the military man in wartime, if the superintendent encountered at Cologne was dressed like the superintendent at Königsberg, and if there was no danger of a Hamburg station inspector being mistaken for a superintendent of the line by someone who has come from Frankfurt.'

Steam's Last Fling

Below: Four engine cleaners pose on an 0-6-0 of the London & South Western Railway at Guildford in about 1920.
Right: The last day of regular steam operation on British Railways (4 August 1968); a 'class 5' at Rose Grove locomotive depot.

Although electric trains had proved themselves in many parts of the world before 1914, and the first diesel locomotive had run its somewhat discouraging trials, steam traction was destined to survive many decades. In Britain, America and on the Continent, the inter-war years may be regarded as the culmination of a century of steam locomotive development, years in which unprecedentedly fast and heavy trains were operated as railways the world over adapted themselves to their new circumstances.

These circumstances were, on the one hand, the erosion of the railways' virtual monopoly in land transport as highway trucks, private cars, and finally airliners emerged as viable carriers. On the other hand, there was a trend towards railway nationalization as many governments decided that railways were too important to be left to the management of private individuals. The threat of nationalization and the consequent need to have good public relations was one factor driving the railways towards greater achievements,

and particularly those which could be readily publicized, like streamlining and fast trains.

In some countries state-owned railways were already an accomplished fact. In Germany, where the individual states had undertaken their own railway systems right from the beginning, it was a short step after World War I to unite them into the all-German *Deutsche Reichsbahn*. In France there already existed one state corporation, the Etat Railway, which was an impecunious company purchased by the government. Elsewhere in Europe some countries had railway systems that were entirely state-owned. In Russia, where most companies were state-owned by 1914, the revolution of 1917 completed the process of nationalization. In Britain the companies had avoided nationalization, but World War I had brought closer some kind of re-structuring.

Superficially, Britain's railways in the war had changed very little. There had been reductions of train services, some facilities like dining cars and sleepers had been withdrawn and women

railway workers had appeared in large numbers. Locomotives tended to be grimy, and some companies had adopted more economical liveries; the Great Eastern and Great Northern painted their locomotives grey, while the Great Western for a time adopted an odious shade of khaki. On a deeper level, however, things could never be the same. The fine wartime performance of the railways, which carried enormously increased traffic often over lines never intended for intensive use, was appreciated by the government and the public, and this fine performance seemed to result from the work of the Railway Executive Committee. The latter was composed of railway managers and coordinated the work of the different companies; that is, it acted as a central directorate. It was this success of a central directing authority, coupled with memories of the negative aspects of the pre-war competition between over 100 different railway companies, that persuaded the British public that the old companies should, in one way or another, be abolished. The result was

the railway amalgamation of 1923, in which four large companies were formed. These companies were the London Midland & Scottish (LMS), whose main constituents were the old Midland, London & North Western, Caledonian, Lancashire & Yorkshire, and Highland railways; the London & North Eastern (LNER), consisting mainly of the Great Northern, North Eastern, North British, Great Eastern, Great Central, and Great North of Scotland railways; the Great Western (GWR) which was the old GWR, alone among pre-war companies in retaining its identity, which absorbed the Cambrian Railway and a few small lines in South Wales; and the Southern Railway (SR), which consisted almost entirely of lines formerly owned by the London & South Western, London Brighton & South Coast, and South Eastern & Chatham railways.

In the USA the railway companies had performed poorly in World War I, so much so that the government felt obliged to take them over. However, the American suspicion of state interference with private enterprise ensured that the companies were restored soon after the War, and they responded to the problems of the future not by merging into larger companies, but by studying ways in which they could avoid a government takeover in the next war. In this endeavour they were successful, for they would work well and in a coordinated fashion in World War II, causing no anxieties to the US Government. In Canada a solution to the state-versus-private company argument was found in the creation of Canadian National Railways, a government corporation which embraced a large number of impoverished lines, with the prosperous Canadian Pacific being allowed to continue as a private company. This was a decision of some genius, for it pleased everybody, even if it did little for the future of railway transport. Those who favoured nationalization were pleased by the new state railway, while those who opposed it were pleased because the Canadian National was obviously destined to be a somewhat unprosperous enterprise and could be made to serve as an example of the evils of state ownership. In France, the private railway companies tried to face their economic difficulties not with radical measures but with requests for government subsidies, and this process continued until they were

Above right: The crest of the London & North Eastern Railway, with the English rose and Scottish thistle among the symbols.
Right: The crest of the Southern Railway, with that Company's interest in electrification properly symbolised.

Above: A Lima 'super-power' 2-8-4 locomotive of the Nickel Plate Railroad.

nationalized in 1938, to form French National Railways (SNCF).

The great problem faced by all railways, nationalized or private, was the increased popularity of the highway truck. After the war, in which the armies had used thousands of motor trucks and worked out better ways of operating and maintaining them, there were many demobilized truck drivers looking for work at the same time as army trucks were being sold off as government surplus. The result was that many small road transport firms sprang up, often consisting of one ex-army truck driver and one ex-army truck. These enterprises naturally went in search of the most highly-paying traffic; that is, they 'skimmed the cream' of the railways' traffic. As the years passed the railways lost more and more of their highly-rated traffic, mostly manufactured goods, and were left with the lower-rated bulk freights like coal and timber.

Obviously this could not go on, and railways in different countries responded differently. In France and Germany they had some success in persuading governments to introduce protective legislation, putting limits on the amount and types of freight carried by motor trucks and imposing higher licence fees on road transport companies. In the USA an effort was made to beat the truckers with improved services. Because the motor truck, which departed as soon as it was loaded and was unloaded as soon as it arrived, and which moreover could move from door to door, offered a faster service to its shippers, the American railways strove to speed up their freight trains and to improve frequencies. In the USA the first of the new truly fast freights was the 'Blue Streak' of the Cotton Belt Railroad, introduced in 1931 and soon imitated by other companies. Such trains helped to stimulate the inter-war American requirement for locomotives of much higher horsepower, capable of moving heavy

freight trains at high speeds. The American locomotive builders had tried various ways to obtain such highpower locomotives, and the most successful was the Lima Locomotive Works, which introduced a range of 'super-power' locomotives having very large fire-boxes supported by four-wheel trucks; that is, 2-8-4 and 2-10-4 locomotives.

The four British railways were rather slow to face the fact that they had lost their monopoly, and when they did they put a great deal of energy into a publicity campaign, asking for a 'square deal' for the railways. They did have a good case. After all, the motor trucks did run on roads provided by the taxpayer, and the railways did have certain burdens which the road transport enterprise escaped: the obligation to publish railway freight rates enabled road transport firms to quote rates which would just undercut those of the railways; another disadvantage, since the railways were legally defined as 'common carriers', was their obligation to carry any traffic

that was offered, while the road carrier could pick and choose. However, although the government was eventually persuaded to introduce some legislation to help the railways it only went part of the way and, with most road transport enterprises consisting of one man and one motor truck, every truck in effect, had a vote.

More useful measures taken by the railways were a speeding up of freight services. The 'express freight', carrying high-value manufactured products in trains fitted with continuous brakes and therefore allowed to travel at higher speeds, ran between major cities at night. The aim was to offer shippers next-morning delivery for freight loaded the previous afternoon. To provide door-to-door facilities without intermediate transhipment, the great advantage of the motor truck, the

Below: A Brunswick-green 'Hall' of the Great Western, with that Company's chocolate-and-cream rolling stock.

railways developed the container. The latter was virtually a freightcar body which could be loaded on to a flatcar for the railway sector of its trip, and on a flatbed truck for the shorter pick-up and delivery sectors. For these fast freights the railways usually made use of 'mixed traffic' locomotives like the 'Halls' of the GWR or the 'Class 5' type 4-6-0 of the LMS, locomotives with driving wheels of about 6ft (1,828mm) which could be used on most passenger trains as well as the fast freight trains. There were also one or two designs built especially for fast freight work. George Churchward's last design for the GWR, his 4700 class 2-8-0, was one such type. 4700 class engines were rarely seen, for they operated on the night freights and spent their days at the locomotive shed.

Despite these measures, British

railways steadily lost their higher-valued freight traffic, and when bulk traffic declined during the Depression o the 1930s their commercial position became difficult. It was not until World War II demonstrated that the railways were still essential that they recovered a measure of self-confidence, only to be nationalized in 1948.

Soon after the motor truck began to make inroads on freight revenue, the private car and the motor coach began to attack passenger revenues. The railways were rather more successful in meeting this threat. Their response was

calculated fare reductions, which in Britain took the form of concessionary day return and excursion tickets, and in the operation of trains so fast that the road competition would be left far behind. In Britain and America these new trains were accompanied by a sustained publicity effort, which persuaded the public that travelling by train was not only faster, but also more glamorous. Streamlining was an ingredient of this public appeal, and the railways deserved great credit for their success in this publicity drive, with its rare achievement of persuading the public that an essentially old form of transport was more fashionable and exciting than a brand new, never-been-done-before, mode.

This public relations success, which among other things aroused the same kind of sporting interest in train performance that the British public had shown during the 'Railway Races' of

Left: The 'Cheltenham Flyer' at speed.
Below: The inaugural 'Silver Jubilee' arrives at London (King's Cross) behind Silver Link. Another A4 stands in the foreground.

1888 and 1895, owed much to the railway engineers and operators, who provided new trains which were quite worthy of the applause they received. The Great Western Railway began this new great age of steam when it retimed its best Cheltenham to London train to run the 77 miles (124km) from Swindon to London in 75 minutes. This was in 1928, and the train was the 'Cheltenham Flyer', hauled by one of the new 'Castle' class locomotives. In later years the 'Cheltenham Flyer' was accelerated, and held the world speed record until it was eclipsed by a Canadian Pacific train in the early 1930s. Meanwhile, the LNER had fitted corridor tenders to some of its new pacific engines, enabling their crews to be changed without stopping and thereby making possible non-stop runs from London to Edinburgh (392 miles or 631km). This, too, was in 1928 and was only the prelude to a burst of renewed competition between the West Coast and the East Coast routes to the north.

In 1935 the first four of the A4 class of streamlined 4-6-2 appeared on the

LNER. These four, painted in an aluminium finish, hauled a similarly aluminium-painted train, the new 'Silver Jubilee', between London and Newcastle (268 miles or 431km) in 240 minutes. Two years later the LMS West Coast Route introduced its own streamlined locomotives, and lively competition followed between new streamliners on the Anglo-Scottish services. The LMS 'Coronation Scot' of 1937 was timed between London and Glasgow (401 miles or 645km) at $6\frac{1}{2}$ hours, while the LNER 'Coronation' ran between London and Edinburgh in 6 hours, covering the first 188 miles (302km) to York at an average of 72mph (116km/h).

Quite apart from the new crack trains, the general run of passenger train services was fast, and many interesting services were introduced. In 1921, for example, Britain's longest through train began to run between Aberdeen and Penzance. In reality, the only part of this train to operate between these two far-distant points was one vehicle, providing a few passenger

The 20th Century, Ltd., between New York and Chicago, 980 miles in 18 hours

enabling passengers to travel overnight without disturbance between London and Paris.

One rather curious achievement of the inter-war years was that of the Great Eastern Railway, in the last year of its independent existence. This was to organize an all-steam commuter service out of its London terminus, Liverpool Street Station, which was intended to show that whatever electric traction could do, steam could do equally well. The quick terminal turnround of the electric multiple unit train was in fact equalled by the Great Eastern operators; this was accomplished by providing the outer end of each platform line with a locomotive siding, so that an incoming train would be followed into the platform by the engine rostered to take it out again to the suburbs on its next departure. This feature, together with carefully worked-out schedules, enabled each set of rails to pass up to twenty-four trains an hour, and each train could carry a thousand

Above: The New York Central Railroad's 'Twentieth Century Limited' speeding over its almost 1,000-mile run between New York and Chicago. The locomotive is one of the Railroad's 'Atlantic' type, which hauled this train prior to World War I.
Right: The blue and silver 'Coronation Scot' leaves London in 1938, hauled by No. 6220, *Coronation*.

compartments and the train guard's accommodation; the remainder of the train was composed of vehicles which were added or detached en route. This was perhaps an extreme example of a characteristic feature of British inter-war train services, the movement in one train of vehicles which would be detached or attached at junctions to provide as many places as possible with through services. Another example was the 'Atlantic Coast Express', the pride of the Southern Railway. This Railway inherited from the London & South Western Railway a number of branch lines in Devon and Cornwall, connecting the main line with various seaside resorts. The 'Atlantic Coast Express' proceeded as a 12-car train from London as far as Devon, and then gradually diminished to the restaurant car and a brake-composite at the end of the last branch line in Cornwall, the remaining vehicles having been detached one by one at preceding junctions and worked to their destination by the respective branchline locomotives. The Southern also inaugurated, in 1936, the first train ferry service between Britain and the Continent. This was the 'Night Ferry', whose sleeping cars were carried by a train ferry between Dover and Dunkirk,

passengers. All this was accomplished with locomotives that were small and quite old, and had the result of postponing electrification of these lines for three decades.

In the USA the railways were rather slow to react to the loss of passengers. In particular, they did little to improve the comfort of the coach passenger, continuing too long to devote their efforts to the further improvement of first class travel. In the 1920s the coach passenger was still furnished with a plush-covered but hardback seat in an open car that was poorly ventilated except when the windows were open! And open windows admitted locomotive smuts. Yet the railroads considered the coach passenger was secure traffic, unlikely to transfer his custom elsewhere. In this they were wrong, and several railroads eventually led the way in offering new inducements. The Baltimore & Ohio Railroad introduced coaches with reclining seats and air-conditioning, while the Chesapeake &

Ohio RR introduced coaches with the usual double row of seats on one side of the aisle, but with only a single row in the other, thereby creating an air of spaciousness usually associated with the first-class-only parlor car. Moreover, when automobiles and motor coaches began to seriously erode the passenger traffic of the eastern railroads at the end of the 1920s, several of the railroads introduced all-coach trains in which, for the first time, parlor cars were available to coach-class passengers.

Trains were not particularly fast in the USA until the early 1930s, although they tended to be longer and heavier. The two rival trains between New York and Chicago, the '20th Century Limited' and the 'Broadway Limited', took 20 hours, even though 18-hour timings had been in force before World War I.

But in 1934 the streamline era on the world's railways was inaugurated by the Union Pacific Railroad's 'M-10000' and the Burlington Railroad's 'Zephyr'. These were both streamlined trainsets

powered by internal combustion engines. These lightweight, high-powered trains carried fewer passengers than conventional trains, but were much faster; when 'M-10000' became the 'City of Portland' it cut the journey from Chicago to Portland to under 40 hours, compared to the 60 hours of the conventional services. It was streamlining, rather than the use of the internal combustion engine, which caught the popular imagination, and other railroads soon introduced their own streamlined trains. These were often conventional trains re-styled to conform to the streamline image, with ordinary steam locomotives covered with a streamlined outer casing. All this activity did succeed in attracting passengers. By 1939, apart from a higher level of comfort, the US railroads offered more than a thousand start-to-stop schedules of over 60mph (96km/h) and despite the advent of the diesel locomotive it was steam locomotives which were the mainstay of these accelerations.

Elsewhere in the world high-speed was pursued less energetically. In France efforts were concentrated on the introduction of diesel railcars, and by 1939 the SNCF had about 650 of these at work. In Germany, where railway passenger traffic remained at a high level despite Hitler's preference for road transport, the high-speed diesel train was developed, culminating in the 'Flying Hamburger' service of 1933. In Australia the state railways did not feel any special measures were needed to hold their passenger traffic, although the Victoria Railways entered the streamline era with a few locomotives specially styled to haul the 'Spirit of Progress' Melbourne-Sydney service as far as the Victoria state border. Meanwhile, on the Trans Australian Railway, opened in 1917 to connect the eastern states with Western Australia, luxurious trains were run, initiating the concept of the rail cruise, which is still offered on this route.

In Britain, the new fast trains were hauled by a new generation of locomotives, designed in the inter-war period and destined to represent the peak of steam locomotive design. On the Great Western, whose engineers were content largely to rest on the laurels of the pre-1914 period, successive variations of George Churchward's designs were introduced. For fast passenger trains, the 'Castle' class was introduced, a larger version of the pre-war 'Star' class of 4-cylinder 4-6-0. This proved to be the Great Western's fastest locomotive, and was built up to the 1950s. The similar but

larger 'King' class was limited to thirty units and reserved for the heaviest trains, especially those between London and Plymouth and London and Wolverhampton. The GWR also evolved the first modern mixed traffic 4-6-0, the 'Hall' class, which was virtually a Churchward two-cylinder passenger locomotive modified with 6ft (1,828mm) instead of 6ft 8½in (2,044mm) driving wheels, giving extra tractive effort for a small sacrifice in speed.

It was a GWR locomotive engineer, William Stanier, who was appointed by the LMS railway as its chief mechanical engineer. On the LMS, friction between different groups of engineers had culminated in the later 1920s with the dominance of the locomotive department by former Midland Railway men. Rather small Midland-type locomotives had been built. The result of this was that Stanier found the LMS locomotive stock inadequate for the new era of faster and heavier trains and began to introduce new designs

Left: A pair of Sydney-built Pacifics haul 'The Spirit of Progress' through New South Wales.
Below left: The Great Western's *Clun Castle*.

incorporating Great Western experience. This transfer of technology was not quite as simple as it may have appeared, and Stanier soon found that GWR practices had to be modified in the light of LMS circumstances, circumstances such as the different type of locomotive fuel, different standards of construction and maintenance. Nevertheless, in the end Stanier did succeed in modifying GWR practices to fit the LMS, and at a time when the GWR was going through one of its less innovative periods his locomotives could be regarded as a further development of the Great Western tradition. In particular, his application of larger superheaters than were used on the GWR was an undoubted success and so, later, was the use of double chimneys; at the very end of its life the GWR itself began to experiment with double chimneys and high-temperature superheat, and found that with these additions its existing locomotive fleet could produce a greatly improved performance. The most spectacular of Stanier's locomotives were perhaps the 'Duchess' class of Pacific, originally

streamlined to haul the 'Corporation Scot'. These were capable of very high power outputs, a great asset when hauling Anglo-Scottish trains up Beattock and other banks. One of them, *Duchess of Hamilton*, carrying the nameplates of the first of the class, *Coronation*, was exhibited in the USA in 1939. This however, was not the first British locomotive to be shipped across the Atlantic for demonstration purposes. A Webb compound had been shown at the Chicago exhibition and the Great Western's *King George V* had been shown at the railway centenary celebrations of the Baltimore & Ohio Railroad in 1930.

Nevertheless, despite the excellence of the 'Duchesses', Stanier's main achievement was the creation of new large classes of locomotive suitable for general duties. Among these were his 8F 2-8-0 and his class 5 4-6-0; both of these were improved versions of GWR designs, the latter being virtually a modified 'Hall'.

Below: The end of the line: two former LMS locomotives await scrapping in the late 1960s.

But in the 1930s the most celebrated locomotives were those designed by Nigel Gresley for the LNER. The earlier of these had been created for the Great Northern Railway, before its incorporation into the LNER, and included the large-boiler Pacifics of which *Flying Scotsman* was the best-known unit (this is another locomotive which has performed on US railroads, but only after its retirement from regular service). Certain locomotives of this three-cylinder design reached very high speeds, sometimes exceeding

100mph (160km/h). When the very similar but streamlined A4 class appeared, even higher speeds were expected. These hopes were not disappointed, for one of this type, *Mallard*, in 1938 broke the official world speed record for steam locomotives, reaching 126mph (203km/h) with a special train. For hauling the fast freight trains which the LNER was accelerating to meet highway competition, Gresley designed what was virtually a smaller version of his 'Flying Scotsman' type of Pacific; this was his 'Green Arrow' 2-6-2,

which during World War II would perform astonishing feats of haulage with very heavy passenger trains. Gresley was a great adherent of the three-cylinder locomotive, and the Gresley valve gear was specially designed for such locomotives. However, this valve gear demanded careful maintenance, and this was not available in the war and post-war years. For this reason, after Gresley's death in 1941 his style of locomotive was not continued in new LNER designs. The latter were less exciting, but rather more reliable in the circumstances.

The Southern Railway between the wars was engaged on a great scheme of electrification, so there was little scope for radical changes in steam locomotive policy. Richard Maunsell, formerly in charge of the locomotives of the South Eastern and Chatham Railway, had become chief mechanical engineer of the Southern and his background, together with the reliance he placed on a chief draughtsman brought up in the Great Western tradition, produced a range of distinctive and highly efficient locomotives. Perhaps the most notable of these were the 40 'Schools' class machines. Designed for the light, frequent, passenger services to the south-east coast, these were a reversion to the 4-4-0 wheel arrangement, and probably the most effective locomotives of this type ever built. In 1940 Maunsell was succeeded by Oliver Bulleid, a former colleague of Gresley, and an engineer for whom innovation was the spice of life. His contribution to the Southern Railway was a fleet of distinctive Pacific type locomotives, beginning with the 'Merchant Navy' class for heavy passenger trains and continuing with the lighter but similar 'West Country' and 'Battle of Britain' series. These had an outer casing which was described not as streamlining, but as air-smoothing, and which was intended less for reducing wind resistance than as a means of making the locomotives suitable for cleaning by mechanical washing installations. Three

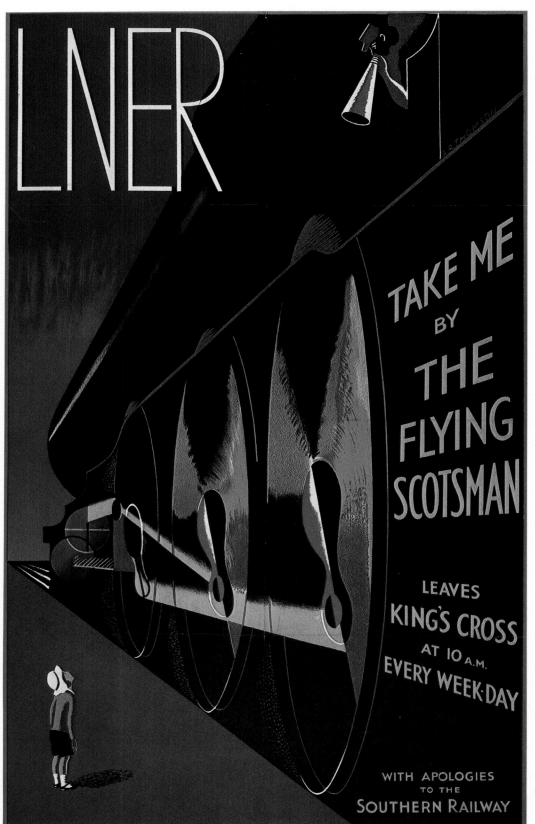

Left: LNER inter-war advertizing, inspired by a well-known Southern Railway poster, recommends the 'Flying Scotsman' train to Edinburgh.
Above right: *Dartmoor*, a Southern Railway 'West Country' 4-6-2 designed by Bulleid as a streamliner but rebuilt by his successors, leaves Bournemouth with a train to Weymouth.
Right: The Canadian Pacific Railway's last standard steam design for heavy passenger trains, the 'Royal Hudson' 4-6-4. The 'Royal' in the name, and the crown insignia, commemorate the use of this class to haul the train of the future King George VI. No. 2856 is shown standing at its locomotive depot in Toronto.

cylinders, chain-driven valve gear, American type disc driving wheels instead of the usual spoked variety, high boiler pressure and great steam-raising capacity were the outstanding features of these locomotives, whose maximum power output was far in excess of normal requirements.

In America high-speed passenger locomotives were frequently a streamlined version of existing types, but new wheel arrangements were favoured. In line with the 'superpower' concept, with four-wheel trucks supporting very large fireboxes, the 4-8-4 and 4-6-4 wheel arrangements became popular. For high-speed service with light trains over winding routes the unusual 4-4-4 arrangement made a brief appearance; the Canadian Pacific Railway made a success of this type, but preferred the 'Royal Hudson' 4-6-4 for its heavier passenger services. The Union Pacific, relying on the 4-8-4 for its main passenger services, achieved success in its endeavour to fit the Mallet type articulated freight engine for fast service. Hitherto the chassis design of these massive and powerful locomotives had made fast running rather risky, but with the 'Challenger' 4-6-6-4 and the subsequent 'Big Boy' 4-8-8-4 (this latter being destined to remain the world's biggest locomotive), a design suitable for both passenger and freight work was

achieved. In the end, the great advantage of this was that such locomotives could be employed on the new accelerated freight services.

In Germany the main locomotive design effort was spent on re-equipping the new Deutsche Reichsbahn with a fleet of standard locomotives. These were built on Prussian principles, high horsepowers taking second place to ease of maintenance and economical operation. In the 1930s, however, Germany joined in the fashion for high-speed locomotives, and built some interesting prototypes, including a 4-6-4 which reached 124mph (199km/h), and a couple of units with 7ft 6in (2,286mm) driving wheels. However, the best-known German locomotive would be the standard 2-10-0, a simplified version of which became the German war service locomotive (*Kriegslok*) in 1939 and served all over occupied Europe where, in some parts, it survives today.

But it was in France that the most astonishing progress in steam locomotive technology was made. In the 1920s André Chapelon showed that, with certain changes, the power output or fuel economy of existing locomotives could be improved by as much as 50 per cent. The modifications he introduced included a carefully calculated exhaust system, using a wider orifice with four jets of steam directed through the chimney, thereby producing a stronger but steadier draught for the fire. Then to an extent greater than that achieved by Churchward, he streamlined the internal steam passages, eliminating the 'throttling' of steam in its passage from

the boiler into the cylinders and out to the chimney. Thirdly, he increased the degree of superheat, so that steam entered the cylinders at the highest temperature possible without burning up the lubricating oil. His first conversion, of a 4-6-2 of the Paris-Orleans Railway, did exactly what he had predicted, producing 50 per cent more power for the same fuel consumption. For the rest of the steam era French locomotive policy was based on Chapelon's principles, a locomotive fleet of highly efficient compound locomotive being created. The only departure from Chapelon principles came with the import of American and Canadian-built mixed traffic 2-8-2 machines after the war. These were two-cylinder units built to a blend of American and French design practices and in which, because of the difficult maintenance problems of that time, the compound system was abandoned.

In Australia, there were sporadic efforts to increase the number of home-built and home-designed locomotives. The Queensland Railway was the most successful in this, introducing locomotives which were a blend of British and US practice. But the other states continued to depend heavily on British locomotive builders. However, the last passenger type to be introduced by the New South Wales Government Railways, the fine green-painted streamlined 3800 series, was designed and built at Sydney during World War II.

Passenger trains in the inter-war years began to contain improved types of rolling stock. Improvements were not

spectacular, but the change to all-metal construction made maintenance easier and provided passengers with better protection in accidents. In America, in particular, the use of aluminium components helped to reduce weight, while in the late 1930s the Budd Corporation's stainless steel bodies, with their strong fluted sides, became a familiar sight on many American railroads. After the war such fluted steel vehicles composed most of the best US trains, and the technique was also used in France. In Britain the most important advance was the mastery of mass-production methods for car-building, an achievement aided by the supercession of wood by steel. Air-conditioning became quite common on US trains after the late 1920s, and the Trans Australian Railway was one of the first non-American railways to adopt it. In many countries on-train telephones, hairdressing saloons and radios were periodically introduced amid great publicity, but never spread beyond a few select trains.

One external change, noticeable especially in America, was the reappearance of more colourful liveries. For years most American railways used a dull olive or brown for their passenger trains, and plain black for their locomotives. The streamline era, however, was embellished by trains and locomotives painted in all colours of the rainbow, and the railroads often employed industrial artists to design both the interiors and the exteriors of their crack trains. In Britain the aluminium finish of the LNER 'Silver Jubilee' and the red and gold of the LMS 'Coronation Scot' were the most remarkable, but in that country these special liveries made less impression because the railways were already using fairly colourful liveries for their passenger services. The Great Western, for example, was still using its dignified Brunswick green and polished brass for locomotives, and chocolate and cream for its passenger trains. The LMS, much to the distaste of its former LNWR employees, chose the Midland Railway's distinctive and beautiful maroon livery for its passenger locomotives and trains, with black for freight locomotives. The LNER used the old Great Northern colours of apple green for passenger locomotives and varnished teak for passenger vehicles. The Southern Railway went through several changes

of different kinds of green before finally settling for a bright deep malachite green, with gold lettering, for its passenger locomotives and trains.

During World War II the railways of the countries at war performed well, often under considerable difficulties. In Britain the emergency train movements arranged at very short notice for transporting soldiers landed after the Dunkirk evacuation functioned faultlessly. The continuation of railway work under bombing became normal, and the effect of air bombardment was much less than had been feared. The German railways suffered badly from bombing in the last months of the war, and transport problems did have an effect on the German war effort. Nevertheless, in relation to the weight of bombs dropped on German railways, the amount of traffic passed through was

surprisingly high; admittedly, though, as in Britain, the number of bombs hitting railway targets was only a fraction of the bombs aimed at those targets. When the war was finished the railway systems of Germany, Russia, France and the Low Countries were in a poor state, physical damage being made worse by the wartime deferment of maintenance. In France and the Netherlands this wholesale destruction was an encouragement to start the large-scale electrification of the railways, and the Netherlands was one of the first countries to entirely dispense with the steam locomotive. However, steam locomotives lasted in France until the 1960s, and longer in Germany and the USSR: indeed, in Eastern Germany it is still possible to see steam locomotives of the inter-war designs, in their original livery of black with red frames and

wheels, hauling mainline trains.

In Britain the four companies created by the railway amalgamation in 1923 came to an end 25 years later, being nationalized to form British Railways in 1948. The four companies had, on the whole, been a success. Only the LMS, the world's biggest railway company, had been so split by internal struggles between supporters of the pre-1923 companies that much of the management's energies was diverted away from the very real commercial and technical problems that it faced. But even the LMS, as time passed, began to pull together.

One of the first acts of the new British Railways management was to hold comparative trials of the different companies' locomotives. That these trials were mishandled (for example, different locomotive crews were given different instructions) did not prevent much useful information being obtained. It was interesting, for example, to learn that Bulleid's Pacifics could put up stirring performances in the Scottish Highlands, and that Gresley's streamlined Pacific, apart from being a very speedy locomotive, came out well in terms of coal and water consumption. Nevertheless, perhaps because former LMS men were in a majority, the new range of British Railways standard locomotives seemed to be very closely related to LMS designs. In terms of performance and fuel economy these locomotives seemed to offer no improvement over pre-war designs, although in some respects, including ease of maintenance, they did have certain advantages. However, it is difficult to refute the claim that the British Railways standard locomotives were quite unnecessary, because existing designs were just as good. The only really outstanding type was the 2-10-0 freight locomotive, which was so well-balanced that it was sometimes used on fast passenger trains. The 4-6-2 passenger locomotive *Britannia* and its sisters also proved to be very competent and their introduction on the former Great Eastern section enabled the main lines from Liverpool Street to introduce a vastly improved train service.

In the mid-1950s, while the construction of the British Railways standard steam locomotives was in full swing, the decision was taken to eliminate steam traction entirely. This combination of circumstances did not reflect great credit on the British Railways management, and the rapid elimination of steam traction was not sound from the economic point of view; the French and the German administrations had been far wiser, keeping steam in service for as long as possible while a step-by-step programme of electrification and dieselization was carried through. In many cases the diesel locomotives purchased by British Railways in their hurried shopping spree proved inferior to the steam locomotives they were intended to replace. Nonetheless, steam traction progressively disappeared from British rails. The last mainline service hauled by steam locomotives was that of the old London & South Western main line from London to the south-west, where Oliver Bulleid's Pacifics, most of them rebuilt to conform with conventional practice, had their last fling. Steam traction on British Railways finally ended in 1968.

This was a decade after the last of the big US railroads, the Norfolk & Western,

One of the Norfolk and Western Railway's streamlined passenger locomotives designed and built in the N. & W.'s Roanoke Shops

Above: Parlor car literature of the 'Powhatan Arrow.' The blotter shows one of the locomotives which hauled this train, the last of the American steam streamliners. **Right:** British Railways' *Britannia* 4-6-2.

had finally abandoned steam traction in favour of diesels. The N & W, being primarily a coal-hauling railroad, resisted the diesel locomotive long after other US companies had made the change, and in the late 1950s was still operating brightly-painted streamlined 4-8-4 locomotives of its own manufacture on passenger trains like the 'Powhatan Arrow'. Elsewhere in North America steam survived on the Canadian Pacific and Canadian National, as well as in Mexico, up to the early 1960s. In many parts of the world the complete changeover to electric or diesel traction came much later. In Australia the last steam trains ran in New South Wales in 1972. In parts of Europe steam traction can still be found; it is still possible with little difficulty to find steam passenger trains in Portugal, Poland, Hungary, East

Germany, Yugoslavia, and Turkey. Moreover, in South Africa, Indonesia, India and China steam locomotives still exist in large numbers. Indeed, in India and China steam units still outnumber electric and diesel. In some quarters this is regarded as a sign of technical backwardness, but it would be fairer to acknowledge that for some countries the steam locomotive is still the most economic form of motive power. It does not demand much capital, it does not burn oil, and it does not demand highly-skilled technicians to maintain it. And even more importantly, it can deliver the goods.

Steam Preserved

Below: The Great Western's *City of Truro*, reputed to have exceeded 100mph (160km/h) in 1904 with the 'Ocean Mail', and now preserved in its birthplace Swindon. Right: *Hardwicke*, a small but doughty 2-4-0 of the LNWR, which participated in the railway 'races' to Scotland.

The railway preservation movement, which has blossomed so widely in many countries over the past two decades, can now be seen to have taken three forms. First there is the railway museum, by far the oldest type of preservation. Then there is the preservation of working exhibits, typically a length of line, closed by its previous owner, which is re-opened by a voluntary organization to operate trains of old-style rolling stock hauled by restored steam locomotives. Lastly, there is 'main-line steam', in which excursions are hauled by steam locomotives on lines still open for normal diesel or electric trains.

The simplest railway 'museum' is the static exhibition of a single locomotive, often in the open air. Several American townships have such an exhibit in their park or outside their station. In the USSR, which has no true railway museum, a number of locomotives which played distinguished parts in World War II are preserved at locomotive depots or stations where they did their war work. However, this kind of preservation requires careful maintenance if the exhibit is not to deteriorate from the weather or from vandalism. In Britain it is a fairly rare form of preservation, although an interesting exception is the display of Robert Stephenson's *Invicta* at Canterbury.

The railway museum at Hamar, in Norway, was probably the first specialized railway museum, and opened in 1896, but Britain was not far behind, for when the North Eastern Railway found itself threatened with the loss of its identity by the 1923 amalgamation it created a museum at York. Initially, this was intended mainly to preserve North Eastern locomotives and equipment, although it has subsequently accepted exhibits from other railways. Until modern times this was Britain's only railway museum. Among its exhibits are the Great Western Railway's *City of Truro*, reputed to have exceeded 100mph (160km/h) in 1904, two of the Great Northern Atlantics, and the London, Brighton & South Coast Railway's *Gladstone*. These were very valuable acquisitions, because they came at a time when little thought was given to preserving obsolete locomotives. Most of the preserved locomotives are of classes that were still in existence when steam traction was being eliminated.

The pioneer days of steam railways are well represented, largely because the Victorians were particularly aware of the significance of the railway age in the mid 19th century – when old colliery locomotives reached the end of their working life, steps were taken to ensure their preservation. Fortunately, Stephenson's *Rocket*, albeit in a somewhat work-worn condition, Hedley's *Puffing Billy* of 1812 and Hackworth's *Sanspareil* (the Rocket's most serious rival at the 1829 Rainhill Trials), are now housed in the Science Museum in London. Other very old locomotives include another Hedley machine in the Royal Scottish Museum, Stephenson's *Locomotion* at York, and Hackworth's *Samson* at New Glasgow in Canada. In Washington, USA, preserved British imported locomotives include Stephenson's *John Bull* of 1831.

In America the Baltimore & Ohio Railroad played a similar role to that of

Britain's North Eastern. Its museum contains locomotives from several railroads, although not unnaturally B & O exhibits predominate. One of the oldest locomotives, Baldwin's *Pioneer* of 1836, is preserved in Chicago. In Germany the Deutsches Museum at Munich and the Nuremburg railway museum have a few old German locomotives, as do museums in most of the other West European countries.

Railway modernization in the last two decades has stimulated further development in railway museums, and several governments, realizing that the steam railway has played such an influential role in social history, have made financial grants available to help acquire exhibits before it becomes too late. Undoubtedly, the outstanding example of the modern railway museum is Britain's National Railway Museum, which opened at York in 1975. Officially a branch of the Science Museum, it is housed mainly in an adapted steam locomotive shed. Its exhibits include not only locomotives, but also old passenger and freight vehicles, signalling equipment, and other small

exhibits. Using its own resources it can restore time-worn acquisitions and return locomotives to working order.

The location of this museum outside the London area was initially opposed, since it was thought that only the capital could provide a worthwhile number of visitors. In fact, the enormous interest and attraction of steam surpassed all expectations, and the new museum received more than two million visitors in its first year. This augurs well for the French railway museum at Mulhouse, which is located in a distant corner of France. The older-established Swiss museum of transport at Lucerne has also not suffered from being situated in a provincial city. However, the new and ambitious Indian railway museum is located in Delhi, while the various railway museums created by railway enthusiasts in Australia are almost all situated close to the state capitals.

In most parts of Western Europe and in the English-speaking world the static museum locomotives are only a small part of the total stock of steam locomotives. Most locomotives are in the hands of various societies, including

those which operate their own tourist railways or organize steam excursions over mainline tracks at weekends. In Britain there is a total of about 350 steam locomotives in existence, and this figure does not include the numerous small industrial locomotives in private ownership. Because the acquisition of locomotives is largely a result of the enthusiasm of private individuals, there has been no overall acquisition policy. This has meant that some types are represented by several units and others not at all. For example, the famous Great Western 'Castle' type is represented by eight units (one of which, *Pendennis Castle*, is in Western Australia). The famous streamlined *A4 Pacific* of the LNER has six representatives, including the record-breaking *Mallard* at York, *Dwight D. Eisenhower* at Green Bay in Wisconsin, and *Dominion of Canada* at Montreal. Because the Great Western Railway had so many devoted supporters, GWR types are in the majority, representing almost 100 of the total. Fewer locomotives of the former London & North Western Railway exist

Above: On the narrow gauge Talyllyn Railway, *Edward Thomas* waits for departure from the Tywyn terminus.
Above left: Two types of GWR tank locomotive, a 2-6-2 and 2-8-0, at work on the Torbay & Dartmouth Railway.
Below left: A former LNER 2-6-0 at work on the North Yorks Moors Railway.
Right: One of the original, and still extant, locomotives of the Talyllyn Railway.

simply because most of that Railway's locomotive types were scrapped before the preservation movement developed.

The idea of a steam tourist railway owed much to the success of a handful of tourist lines built at a time when the steam locomotive was still in its prime. There were mountain railways in Switzerland, Mount Washington, and Snowdon, which made their money solely by carrying tourists. There were also a few narrow gauge lines built as tourist attractions near popular holiday resorts. These seaside or scenic railways included the lengthy 1ft 3in (380mm) gauge Romney, Hythe and Dymchurch Railway in southern England and the Ravenglass & Eskdale Railway in Cumbria. Both these lines are still operating with steam locomotives specially built for them.

However, the great inspiration for railway preservers is the Talyllyn Railway in Wales, the first of the modern generation of tourist lines. This railway, penetrating into the slate area of central Wales from the harbour of Towyn, has had a long life; it was originally built in 1865 to take slate from the quarries to the harbour. Of 2ft 3in (685mm) gauge, the line had two locomotives and, despite the slump in the slate industry, managed to remain in existence until 1950, thanks to an owner who preferred to make a loss rather than to close it. However, when the owner died closure seemed inevitable until a group of dedicated railway enthusiasts decided to revive it as a passenger carrier. This was the world's first privately preserved railway, and to a large extent this endeavour depended initially on how determined and successful their fund-raising activities were.

Eventually the Railway was restored and, with its original locomotives once more running along its tracks, passenger services were advertized in the hope of attracting sightseers to the Abergynolwyn Valley, through which the line passed. Until that stage it had been hard to calculate just how much traffic there would be (a common experience of railway entrepreneurs right from the very start of the railway age), but as things turned out there was enough traffic to justify all the efforts put into the re-opening. Over the years this traffic has increased as old clients return and new ones hear about the line's attractions; more locomotives have been acquired from other, extinct, narrow gauge lines, and the restored length of the Railway has been extended.

The narrow-gauge preservation movement in Wales has since taken its own distinct course. There are now so many lines that it has become feasible to join forces for advertizing purposes, 'The Great Little Trains of Wales' slogan being one result. It seems that a

multiplicity of lines in one area can increase, rather than decrease, the traffic of a given line, because many more people are attracted by the prospect of 'doing' several lines in one trip. Two of the Welsh steam narrow gauge lines are not, strictly, preserved, because they have performed their original purpose without a break and without needing revival by volunteer organizations. These are the ever-profitable Snowdon Mountain Railway, and the Vale of Rheidol Railway. The latter is British Rail's only steam operated line, and was inherited from the Great Western Railway at the time of nationalization. A very different Welsh line is the Welshpool & Llanfair, a former country line serving an agricultural district not far from the border with England. Revived by a dedicated body of volunteers, this line is now being extended back over its original route to Welshpool. It is very much a working museum of narrow gauge locomotives, the original *Earl* and *Countess* now being supplemented by

several other locomotives, including a German military railway's 0-8-0 tank locomotive of World War II, a modern 2-6-2 from the now closed Sierra Leone Railway in West Africa, and an elderly sugar plantation locomotive from the West Indies. Despite this overseas flavour, the line somehow succeeds in maintaining the countrified atmosphere of the original W & L.

The biggest of the Welsh narrow gauge enterprises is the Festiniog Railway, which was re-opened for tourist traffic by its preservation society in 1955. Another former quarry line, it had once been the bright new hope of the narrow gauge concept; in the 1870s delegations from several countries had visited it to see its Fairlie single or double-boiler locomotives at work. These flexible or articulated wheelbase machines which spread the weight of a locomotive, seemed to promise great haulage capacity for the narrow gauge,

Above: A Fairlie double-boiler locomotive of the Festiniog Railway.

encouraging the hope that the narrower gauges could be built in poorer parts of the world instead of the more expensive broader gauges. The Fairlie locomotive in practice did not quite justify these hopes, being rather difficult to maintain in steam-tight order, but the present-day Festiniog Railway still uses two of these unique locomotives, having rebuilt the original units in its own workshops. Apart from being the biggest, the Festiniog is the most commercial of the Welsh lines, and at times has seemed to be in danger of over-commercialization. But with passenger traffic now around 400,000 annually (concentrated in the summer months when the line is open) some degree of organization more efficient than that traditionally associated with narrow gauge railways is unavoidable. In the summer the line runs four train-sets on peak-days, so there is scope for the employment of a sizeable locomotive fleet. Apart from the

Fairlies, the line has two locomotives which once worked at the Penryn Quarry in North Wales, and also *Mountaineer,* a 2-6-2T built in America for service in France during World War I.

The role of volunteer labour in these early schemes was crucial. All available money had to be spent on materials and equipment; wages were out of the question. In most cases the amount of work involved was underestimated. Indeed, had some preservation societies fully realized what lay ahead of them they would probably have abandoned their plans. Restoring a railway which has not been used for years is no light endeavour. The rails and sleepers might still be in place, but thick thorny vegetation, blocked drainage, subsidence and landslip, and rotting sleepers together provide a daunting obstacle to men unused to physical labour and equipped with little apart from spades, saws and axes. Interestingly, it is this kind of arduous work that has been most attractive to volunteers, possibly because it gives an

opportunity for them to work themselves to a state of exhaustion amid fresh air and unspoiled scenery. Many of the larger societies have a nationwide organization, and local groups may specialize in their tasks. On the Festiniog Railway, for example, there is an area group in Lancashire which sends working parties for tracklaying, another in Staffordshire which specializes in fencework and another at Leicester whose 'homework' has been the restoration of derelict rolling stock.

Obtaining serviceable rail and sleepers has been a problem. In the 1960s, when British Railways was closing hundreds of miles of line, it was easy to buy good second-hand trackwork at a cheap price, but the situation has changed over the last few years. On the narrow gauge lines the sleeper problem is perhaps easier, because old mainline sleepers can be sawn up to provide two narrow gauge sleepers. Wisely, even though perhaps inevitably, there has been little attempt to reproduce old-style track. Whatever

components are available are used, and on some lines it is possible to see sections laid with like-new secondhand flatbottom rail acquired from government stocks built up during World War II for military railways, laid on Australian Jarrah-wood sleepers and attached by the same kind of clips as are used on British Rail's main lines.

As the early Welsh narrow gauge ventures were getting into their stride, British standard gauge preservation began. In 1960 two pioneer lines appeared. One was the famous Middleton Railway, where Matthew Murray's steam locomotives had worked in 1812. This was to remain unique among preserved lines, at least in Britain, because although it runs steam passenger services in summer its main traffic is freight. The other 1960 line was much more ambitious, and its success inspired similar ventures. This was the railway which called itself the Bluebell Railway. Originally part of a branch line of British Railways from Horsted Keynes to Lewes in Sussex, it was closed in 1959 against strong local opposition. It was

this opposition that initiated the scheme for a privately-operated line, which has now become the 5-mile (8-km) Bluebell Railway. This railway has also prospered, and now owns a large collection of working steam locomotives.

Being a pioneer, the preservation society organizing the Bluebell Railway could call on little past experience to help it resolve the many legal issues which confronted it. But as with all preservation societies, the membership includes a very wide range of talents and professions, including lawyers. Making use of 19th century legislation designed for very different ends, the society formed itself into a limited company, and then applied to the Ministry of Transport for a Light Railway Order (a procedure originally designed to encourage agricultural railways). After this, a further application was made for a light railway transfer order,

transferring the line, at a price, from British Railways to the new company.

Later preserved railways followed similar procedures. Although each of the many preserved lines had its own individuality, there was a typical sequence of events. What usually happened was that when British Rail proposed to close a little-used but much-loved line there was a local protest movement which, having failed to prevent closure, then formed a society to re-open the line. A fund would be raised and volunteers registered. Fund-raising was often a hurdle which some societies never cleared; appeals for donations would meet with a disappointing response unless there was brilliant salesmanship. The sale of shares in the new company was sometimes more successful, but not always. But if enough money and volunteers were collected, the mammoth task of clearing the track and repairing structures began. A few lucky railways with the right connections sometimes persuaded territorial army units to devote their summer camp to

Below left: Smokebox soot removal at the Haworth locomotive depot of the Keighley & Worth Valley Railway.

working on their line. After some track had been cleared, and preferably when a working locomotive was available, the society or company would begin to hold 'gala days' to which the public was invited. It was the response to this invitation which often determined the fate of the enterprise; a good public attendance not only raised money but also brought the wide local publicity and interest which the railway needed. If the public did indeed show its interest, the railway could apply for a Light Railway Order, allowing it to run public passenger services, subject to certain safety and operating requirements. If this public passenger service was well patronized it would be extended from an occasional weekend service to a summer service, perhaps running every day of the week with extra trains at weekends. By which time volunteer labour became inadequate, and permanent staff were needed.

At this stage, a railway running a summer passenger service and making an operating profit still had its problems. Being essentially a working

museum, it had to use 'exhibits' for its trains, and inevitably these slowly wore out. Replacing worn parts became increasingly difficult as components were no longer made by former locomotive building companies; each had to be a special order, unless the railway's own volunteers could muster the design and manufacturing talent to make their own, which they often did. But the time must come when a locomotive needs to be rebuilt, and the question arises of whether it then ceases to be a true museum piece. In future it seems quite likely that entirely new locomotives may be built by or for the more prosperous preserved lines. Indeed, a new copy of Stephenson's *Locomotion* was built for the celebration in 1975 of the 150th anniversary of railways and in 1979 working replicas of the locomotives participating in the Rainhill trials were built for a re-enactment of these trials during the 150th anniversary celebrations of the Liverpool & Manchester Railway.

Maintenance of steam locomotives to meet the requirements of the Board of

Trade's safety inspectors is also expensive, requiring the frequent replacement of boiler tubes. In short, a preserved railway needed not only to make an operating profit, but also to make enough revenue to enable a capital fund to be established for the acquisition or reconstruction of locomotives in the future.

It would be too much to expect that the peculiar situation in which a preserved railway is 'shared' by an owning/operating company and a supporters' association of volunteers would be free of acrimony. In fact some railways have, at times, been almost torn apart by internal dissension, although such crises seem to be very short, ending in a return to tolerance and compromise. One possible source of discord, especially in the early years, was that a locomotive belonging to an individual might be restored by volunteers who, for nothing, would enhance the value of the locomotive by their devoted labours; the owner would then be free to do what he liked with his locomotive, even sell it at a profit. Such cases were very rare, and moreover even in the worst case the volunteers had achieved their main object, the restoration of a valued piece of machinery. Nowadays a more common, and perhaps inevitable, cause of friction is the difference of aim between the company (intent on attracting paying passengers) and the volunteers (wishing to create and operate an authentic old-time railway). This can lead to stormy dissension if the company decides to provide 'public attractions' inconsistent with the authenticity of the line. For example, a Devonshire line representing a typical Great Western branch line aroused a minor storm when it decided to attach nameplates to locomotives which in their previous career had never carried them. Another line was criticized when it painted a locomotive of pre-nationalization design in pre-nationalization colours, because that particular locomotive had been built after nationalization.

One reason why steam locomotive preservation has developed further in Britain than in other countries is that a scrapyard in South Wales, which purchased withdrawn locomotives up to the end of steam, retained most of them for years and in 1979 still had a few rusting away on its storage tracks. This provided the time needed by preservation societies to gather their forces before buying their locomotives. Obviously, once a locomotive has been bought and moved by road to its new owners' premises, there is an enormous amount of work to be done before it can become a 'runner'. One of the last locomotives to be returned to service is *Duke of Gloucester*. The recent history of this locomotive is interesting not only because it is fairly typical of the sequence which preservation societies have to follow, but also because it throws some interesting light on British locomotive design and construction.

Duke of Gloucester was the last passenger locomotive design of British Railways, and was the sole representative of its class. Built at a time when British Railways was engaged in a somewhat unwise programme of steam locomotive building, it was intended to represent the very best in modern design and construction. In particular its steam distribution through Caprotti poppet valve gear was said to make it the most efficient locomotive to run on British rails. Its crews did not share this

opinion, but did not complain too loudly. Because it was built at a time when the immediate future belonged to the diesel locomotive, it had a very short life, but after withdrawal it was scheduled for official preservation by British Railways. However, there were second thoughts and the locomotive was sold for scrap, just its outside cylinders and their sophisticated valve gear being preserved for posterity. Not long afterwards a preservation society was formed to save this locomotive, its members being predominantly men with an interest in engineering. In 1974, after the purchase price of almost £5,000 had been paid, the locomotive left the scrapyard for five years of restoration. Thanks to the varied engineering and draughting skills of its members, much of the work could be done cheaply, but a few firms contributed free components, while other spare parts were collected from as far away as Malaysia (whose locomotives had also used Caprotti valve gear). As for the boiler, this was stripped of its cladding, sand blasted, and treated with anti-rust phosphoric acid to restore its external condition, while its interior received new tubes. Most of the main parts of the locomotive, like the cab, wheels, axles, boiler and frames, were detached, cleaned and repaired. However, replacing the missing outside cylinders and their valve gear was a near-impossible undertaking because the original drawings were not obtainable.

Eventually the society's draughtsmen set to work, using drawings of other smaller Caprotti designs and checking with *Duke of Gloucester*'s original valve gear on view in the Science Museum. Just as this work was completed, the National Railway Museum found the original drawings; comparison of the two showed that the 'amateurs' had produced drawings that were identical with the professionals' originals.

The ashpan being in poor repair, a new one was made. Again, the society's draughtsmen produced the drawings, taking the old ashpan as a model. When these drawings were compared with the originals, again unearthed a little too late, it was found that the damper doors of the new drawing were considerably smaller than those of the original drawing. This led to the conclusion that the original ashpan had been wrongly built; since this meant that the access of air to the fire was considerably more constricted than the designers had intended, it explained why in its mainland service this locomotive had seemed unable to produce a very high output and was frequently the despair of its fireman. Thus one cause of the locomotive's disappointing performance was discovered. Equally disturbing was what seemed to be another cause of the locomotive's inadequacy; the Caprotti Company had specified that the locomotive should have the Kylchap chimney arrangement, which was most suited to poppet valve gears. But British

Above left: Restoration of a former British Railways' 2-10-0 on the Bluebell Railway in 1979.
Right: One of the world's most celebrated locomotives, this Stanier 'Black 5' 4-6-0 is being broken up for scrap.

Railways had fitted its own version of blastpipe and chimney, which was probably less suitable for this locomotive. Thanks to gifted and enthusiastic amateurs, therefore, the re-born *Duke of Gloucester* will have an air inlet and steam outlet more in keeping with its reputation as the last word in British steam locomotive design.

There are over 100 preservation societies belonging to the Association of Railway Preservation Societies in Britain, so a complete listing is impracticable here. Many are quite small, owning perhaps a half-restored locomotive which they hope to operate one day on the preserved line of another society or even over the tracks of British Rail. Some own a length of abandoned track which they hope to clear for use by locomotives and trains which they do not yet possess. At times, so many aspiring preservation societies have been raising enthusiasm and funds that it seemed likely that a modern version of the Railway Mania was being enacted. But in spite of all the difficulties, a surprising number of apparently no-hope enterprises eventually established themselves, and it would be rash to predict the failure of any particular scheme. Meanwhile, the larger societies seem to go from strength to strength, carrying more passengers each season. A few maintain some kind of skeleton service throughout the year, while a larger number now re-open for a short period around Christmas.

The two lines operated in Devon by the Dart Valley company are a good example of a deliberate and successful attempt to reproduce the form and atmosphere of a particular railway. Both the Paignton-Kingswear and Buckfastleigh-Totnes lines of this enterprise were originally Great Western branch lines, although the former could be regarded as a continuation of the main line. These lines have prospered, and provide opportunities for the regular running of a number of Great Western locomotives.

Another line with a distinctive company atmosphere is the Keighley & Worth Valley Railway in Yorkshire, which has a locomotive stock in which former LMS types predominate. Not far from Birmingham, a source of both volunteer labour and passengers, the Severn Valley Railway operated part of a former Great Western secondary line with locomotives which originated mainly on the Great Western or the LMS. Here, too, the Great Western architecture and general style has been well preserved. As for the old Southern

Railway, apart from the Bluebell Railway there is the relatively new 'Watercress' line in Hampshire, where a former London & South Western Railway line has been re-opened. The LNER, which has been less well-served by the preservation societies, is represented on the North Yorkshire Moors Railway, a line of the former North Eastern Railway. This line also seems to prosper even though it is off the main tourist route.

Many of the preservation societies have benefitted from the support of local authorities. In Wales, for example, the Welsh Tourist Board has done much to assist the narrow-gauge lines, both by offering publicity and, sometimes, funds. Probably the most notable example of such cooperation, however, is to be found at Peterborough, home of the Nene Valley Railway. The establishment of a railway society here coincided closely with the first moves to create a 'new town' at Peterborough.

The Development Council planned an extensive recreation area on the present outskirts of the town, which in due course would be close to the centre of the new town. As a result the Peterborough Railway Society's idea of a steam railway for five miles along the Nene Valley, passing through the proposed park, was welcomed, and consequently the Development Council agreed to buy the disused line from British Rail and lease it to the Society. To begin with steam locomotives from the neighbouring British Sugar Corporation's railway were used, but these have since been supplemented by others. What nowadays makes the Railway so notable is its extensive use of non-British locomotives. This began

Below: The locomotive yard at Haworth of the Keighley & Worth Valley Railway, with a 'class 5' in the foreground.
Bottom: Continental atmosphere on the Nene Valley Railway: an ex-German 2-6-2 tank locomotive at the head of a train.

when a Swedish tank locomotive, in excellent condition as it had been part of the Swedish strategic reserve, was put for sale at an attractive price. It was concluded that to bring the line to the continental European standard for lineside clearances required the alteration only of two structures, which were due for renovation in any case, so the locomotive was bought. This has since been followed by other European locomotives, including a Danish 0-6-0 tank and one of the celebrated Du Bousquet compound locomotives of the former Nord Railway of France. The latter is one of the most celebrated locomotive types ever built, and its preservation in working order is most valuable for a generation which otherwise would have no opportunity of witnessing a French compound locomotive in action.

Another line which operates foreign machines is the Main Line Steam Trust, based in Loughborough and utilizing a section of the former Great Central Railway main line. This regularly runs a beautifully restored Norwegian Railways 2-6-0. In this case, as with the Nene Valley Railway, British enthusiasts have made a supplementary contribution to the work of the sometimes rather weak preservation movements abroad. In this connection mention should also be made of the Steamtown enterprise at Carnforth in Cumbria. This, among its predominantly British locomotives, has a German Pacific and a French compound Pacific of the 231K class; however, these locomotives cannot be operated within the confines of the British loading gauge. One or two American engines are also preserved in Britain. Apart from the war-time narrow-gauge unit used by the Festiniog Railway, there are several of the 0-6-0 shunting tank locomotives used by the American army in World War II. Also, recently bought from the Polish railways is a 2-8-0 of the well-known US Transportation Corps design. Being designed for overseas service in the first place, these US army locomotives are not restricted by clearance problems. It seems possible that further foreign locomotives will be acquired. The expense of transport is compensated by the better condition of locomotives which have been in reserve or in supervised storage, rather than standing in the open for several years. The movement is not entirely one-way; there is a tourist line in North America, which some years ago bought a British 'Schools' class 4-4-0 which is now operated on excursions, and in Australia there is the Great Western *Pendennis Castle*. Some of the American railway museums have British and Irish

Above: SNCF No. 231K 22, now preserved in England, awaits departure at Calais.

locomotives as static exhibits, while the Delson museum near Montreal includes a Gresley Pacific as well as an old French 0-6-0.

Steamtown at Carnforth, a very commercial enterprise, is an example of a preservation site developed without any original intention of running trains on a stretch of line. Instead, it was intended to use the old British Railways locomotive depot at Carnforth as, simply, a motive power museum, with locomotive running being confined to short movements in the shed yard. As things have turned out, locomotives from this site have been used on excursions over British Rail. A somewhat similar situation has come into being at Birmingham, where the Standard Gauge Steam Trust, based at the former Tyseley locomotive depot, stages not only 'open days' but also organizes excursions with its collection of former Great Western locomotives. At Bressingham in Norfolk there is also a large display of locomotives, including Royal Scot and a French, American-built, 2-8-2. These locomotives are on display and also run short distances under their own power as part of an exhibition. Another locomotive depot site, run more for pleasure than profit by the Great Western Society, is at Didcot, near Oxford. Here the old Great Western locomotive depot still houses Great Western locomotives, the property of the Society. Beautifully restored, some of this Society's locomotives occasionally grace British

Rail tracks with week-end excursions; the Society also has a set of chocolate-and-cream Great Western passenger vehicles.

From time to time the preserved lines have attempted to diversify their traffic, so as to reduce their dependence on the tourist. The Nene Valley Railway sometimes handles freight traffic, and the Dart Valley once provided a train for schoolchildren throughout the school year, as does the Romney, Hythe and Dymchurch. The West Somerset Railway, based at Minehead, has been exceptional in this respect, because it was intended to be a public service railway as much as a tourist line right from the beginning. Its long-term objective is to run the full length of the old Great Western branch from Minehead to Taunton, and only financial and political constraints have so far prevented this; neither British Rail nor the railway trade unions have been very encouraging in this endeavour. The railway, a relatively recent arrival, at first confined its operations to the Minehead-Watchet section, where there was both local and tourist traffic potential. More recently it has rehabilitated the railway further inland, towards Taunton. It is an all-the-year-round operation, using a secondhand British Rail diesel multiple unit train for its local passenger traffic and one of its three active steam tank locomotives for its weekend steam trains during the summer. Many of its shares were bought by local inhabitants, interested not so much in railway preservation but in good local transport.

After Britain, the USA is the country

with the most developed pattern of steam operated tourist lines. Partly this is because at the time when steam traction was disappearing there were many wealthy Americans who could afford to buy old locomotives and track from their own resources, without spending time and energy on forming societies to raise money. However, this has meant that very often preserved lines are dependent on one person, and are liable to cease operations on his death, bankruptcy, or loss of interest. In a sense the USA was a pioneer of the tourist line, for the Edaville Railroad was opened in 1947. However, at that time it was more to satisfy the whim of its owner, a cranberry farmer who intended that this narrow gauge line should serve his farm. Based on the much loved Maine 'Two-footers' and using much equipment from those defunct 2ft (610mm) gauge lines, the Edaville Railroad unexpectedly attracted the general public, and soon began to operate passenger trains for tourists at holiday times. Another one-man foundation was Steamtown at Bellows Falls in Vermont. Like the Edaville Railroad it combined static with working exhibits, although in this case it was a standard gauge operation and the track was not specially laid, the steam excursions operating over the Green Mountain Railroad, a tourist line using trackage formerly belonging to the Rutland Railroad.

Another long-established tourist line, the Strasburg Railroad, was also originally a rich man's hobby. One of the USA's many 'short lines', it was facing abandonment in 1958, since its original freight traffic had fallen victim to the motor truck. Its purchasers intended to renovate it as a kind of hobby, but in the expectation that they could revive its freight traffic. However, the freight was not forthcoming, so the expected revenue had to be obtained elsewhere; hence the decision to operate a steam tourist service. This 4½ mile (7km) line passes through the agreeable landscape of Pennsylvania's 'Dutch Country', and this, together with the prospect of travelling behind a steam locomotive, has proved enormously popular. Some freight is still carried, giving an authentic touch to the Railway. Its locomotives include a former Canadian National 0-6-0 switch engine, and an attractive 4-4-0 formerly belonging to the Pennsylvania Railroad. Subsequently, one or two other short lines supplemented their freight operations with steam passenger trains. A notable revival was that of the Arcade & Attica Railroad in New York State, which acquired a 4-6-0 and 2-8-0 to

Above: A Mallet tank locomotive at work on the Vivarais Railway in France.

haul its weekend passenger runs.

Possibly the best-known of the American tourist lines is that of the Silverton Railroad, a 3ft (915mm) gauge line of 45 miles (72km) which was once part of the Denver & Rio Grande RR's narrow gauge network in the Rockies. It is still operated by that Railroad, but its service is confined to the summertime daily round-trip tourist run, hauled by one of the line's original 2-8-2 locomotives. Since its opening as a tourist attraction, considerably aided by the state government, traffic has developed so well that two thirds of the passenger cars are of new construction. Also in the Rockies, the states of New Mexico and Colorado have sponsored another long 3ft (915mm) gauge tourist operation, that of the 64 mile (103km) Cumbres & Toltec Scenic RR.

State sponsorship is not unusual. In West Virginia, for example, the Cass Scenic Railroad was created by the State from the remains of a standard gauge logging railroad. With its steep gradients, switchbacks, and the once-so-common geared steam locomotives, it is a good reproduction of how forestry

railroads once worked in the USA.

Most countries in western Europe have one or two preserved steam railways. In some cases, the preservation movement started in earnest only when most locomotives had already been scrapped. In France, for example, there is a shortage of locomotives suitable for hauling steam excursions. Nevertheless, France does possess some very attractive lines. One of the oldest is the Pithiviers line, not far from Paris. This is an old sugar beet line built on the Deceauville 2ft (609mm) gauge system. The locomotives and stock now used are also mainly from Deceauville lines and the whole enterprise provides a very good representation of what narrow gauge agricultural railways, once so common in France, really looked like. Also in France the AJECTA society operates a weekend steam train to Richelieu in Touraine over an SNCF branchline still used on weekdays for regular freight service. A 2-6-0 of the former Est Railway is the mainstay of this standard

Above: An American-designed, Australian-built locomotive of the 'Puffing Billy' Railway.

gauge service. In the Massif Central there is the Vivarais Railway, a still-operating remnant of an extensive metre-gauge system, once one of France's many local railways. A feature of this line, apart from the mountain scenery, is the use of the line's original Mallet type tank locomotives, which, in the tourist season haul trains of up to twelve vehicles.

Holland and Switzerland both have several tourist lines. That of Hoorn-Mademblik in Holland is especially interesting because it also carries considerable freight traffic. The Dutch lines use mainly German-built tank locomotives. In Germany itself the preservation movement is still developing. The usual practice is for preservation societies to concentrate on the acquisition and restoration of vintage locomotives and rolling stock, which are operated at weekends on still-open freight lines.

Australia's best-known preserved line is the 'Puffing Billy' 2ft 6in (750mm) gauge line from Belgrave, near Melbourne. Once part of the Victoria narrow gauge railway system, this enterprise, founded in 1954, still uses the original 2-6-2 tank locomotives, designed by Baldwin in America but built in Australia. In this case the Victoria Railways still maintain control, and provide the key operating staff, but volunteers perform most tasks. In New Zealand the 'Kingston Flyer' is entirely a state railway affair. This vintage train, hauled by an elderly Pacific locomotive, has been a great success, although only introduced quite recently.

The 'Kingston Flyer' really represents another variety of preserved steam operation, the use of steam locomotives on mainline railways. In Britain this pattern had its origins before the steam locomotive was threatened by the diesel. In 1938, for example, an old Great Northern 'single' was brought out of retirement to haul a few excursions from London. Then in the 1950s, British Railways refurbished a handful of museum locomotives. These were intended to haul excursions, but were attached to locomotive depots like normal locomotives and took their share of normal traffic. Thus the veteran Great Western 4-4-0 *City of Truro* could be seen regularly hauling a stopping train between Swindon and Bristol. In subsequent years, and especially after the end of steam on British Railways, steam excursions have run on a few selected main lines in Britain, using privately owned locomotives. These excursions brought revenue to both British Rail and to the societies that sponsored them. So promising was public response that in 1978 British Rail decided to introduce its own regular steam trains, running on certain days throughout the summer, and using locomotives that were either privately preserved or the property of the National Railway Museum.

In the USA mainline steam excursions have been irregular, because so much has depended on the availability of locomotives and the willingness of railway companies to accept steam excursions on their tracks. Attitudes vary from management to management, and in any case it is expensive to keep heavy steam locomotives in service. The

Southern Railway has been particularly hospitable, and has kept 2-8-0 and 2-8-2 locomotives of its own for use on excursions. Another occasional performer has been 8444, one of the massive 4-8-4 passenger locomotives of the Union Pacific RR. At one time a Nickel Plate 2-8-4, No 759, was often used. For the 'Freedom Train' that toured the USA in the Centennial year of 1976 Southern Pacific and Reading RR 4-8-4 locomotives were used, and there can be little doubt that despite the difficulties, heavy steam locomotives will continue to make an appearance at the head of special trains. North of the border the Canadian National has been a willing sponsor of steam trips, using its own locomotive. In recent years it has kept one of its more modern steam locomotives, 4-8-2 No. 6060, in service for this purpose. In this case the Railway expects to benefit from favourable publicity and this is one of the motives for the operation by several Australian state railways of their own 'vintage trains'. These trains, consisting of old passenger cars with a suitably old locomotive, participate in local celebrations, like the centenaries of various townships, and are thus seen by many Australians in outlying areas. In Australia, too, the state railway enthusiast organizations arrange their

own steam excursions, using either their own locomotives or those preserved by the state railways.

In France in recent years steam excursions have been hauled by the solitary available standard gauge steam locomotive, a 4-6-0 of the former Paris-Orleans Railway. Although this situation may change, for an American-built 2-8-2 will probably become available, there is little prospect of much variety in locomotive power on French excursions. In Germany the situation is very different; many locomotives have been preserved but the state railway (DB), is reluctant to accept them on its lines. One solution has been to arrange German steam excursions over the rails of the nearby and more hospitable Netherlands Railways.

In most countries the steam preservation movement has increased far beyond the hopes of its earliest adherents. But there must come a time when too many projects dilute to a crippling degree the available traffic. Also, many of these lines have not yet solved their long-term equipment problems. Providing covered accommodation for their elaborately restored rolling stock is unexciting and expensive, but must be done. Provision for rebuilding worn-out locomotives must be made out of

revenue. Something has to be done to replace the ageing generation of locomotivemen who have the experience needed to handle steam excursions. Above all, public interest must be maintained; passenger traffic has on most railways been fast to develop, but this may have been because present-day heads of families belong to that generation which, having been brought up in the steam age, now wishes to share its pleasures with the children. But on the preserved lines there is already a contingent of young volunteers who are too young to have known regular steam trains, so evidently previous experience is no bar to the growth of enthusiasm. It is also noteworthy that as the first diesel locomotive types are sent to the scrapyards, a diesel preservation movement has begun to flourish. On the railways, it seems, anything that is disappearing attracts its admirers and preservationists. Already one or two railway preservation groups have added an obsolete diesel locomotive to their steam stock, and this is a trend which seems likely to continue.

Index

Acknowledgements

The publishers would like to thank the following organizations and individuals for their kind permission to reproduce the photographs in this book:

Bodleian Library 53; British Tourist Authority 7 below left, 52; Jean-Loup Charmet 1, 40, 42, 51, 60; Colourviews Picture Library 23 below, 25, 70–71, 80, 83 above, 92; Cooper-Bridgeman Library endpapers, 7 centre, 13 below right, 14 above, 17, 21 below. 31 above and below, 46, 47, 54–55 below; Ehrlich Tweedy Archive 48, 68 above, 72 above, 83 below; Mike Esau 26, 65, 82 below, 86–87; Mary Evans Picture Library 27 below, 57, 59; Chris Gammell 24 below, 33, 81, 84, 93; Colin Garratt 2–3, 4–5, 37, 73, 75 above right, 89; Victor Goldberg 29 above left, 34, 41, 43 below, 49, 70; J M Jarvis 27 above,

67, 75 below, 85, 90 below right; Leicester County Museum 20; Mansell Collection 12, 43 above, 45; Merseyside County Museum 10; J G Moore Collection 23 above; Nation Railway Museum 29 right, 30, 32, 56, 58, 61, 63, 66 above and below, 74, 77; Photo History 24 above right. Photographic Library of Australia 94; Rail Archive Stephenson 64, 69, 82 above, 88, 90 above right, 91, 95; Ann Ronan Picture Library 9 above left; Santa Fe Railway 44; Science Museum 6 below left and right, 7 above left, below left, 13 below left, 14 below, 15, 18, 50; Smithsonian Institution 19; John Topham Picture Library 28, 36; Union Pacific Railroad Museum Collection 21 above; United States Information Service 8; Verkehrmuseum (Nuremberg) 16; Vision (Chris Kapolka) 72 below, 79; John Westwood 35, 54–55 above, 68 below, 76, 78; Zefa (J M Jarvis) 38–3

PDO 81-290

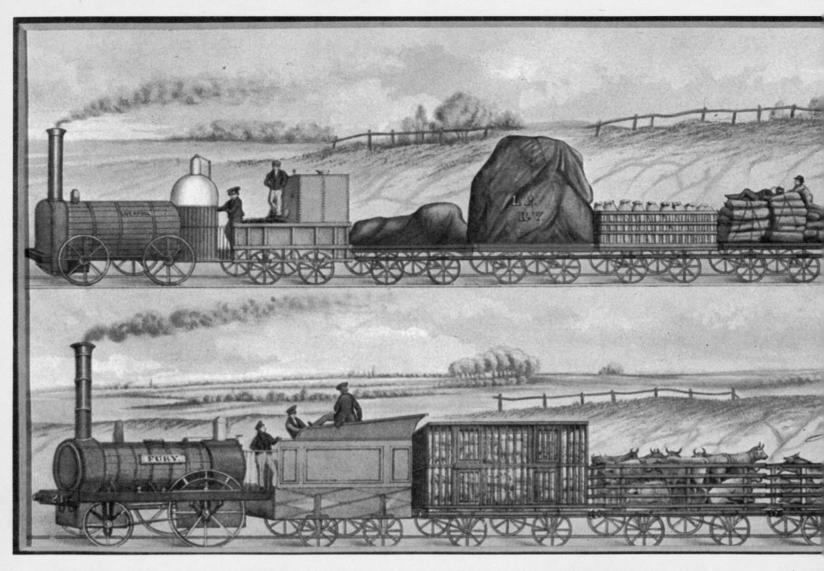